The Feasts and The Future

The Cross to New Creation Foreshadowed in Israel's Feasts

James F. Bender

and

Daniel G. Fuller

Copyright © 2016 James F. Bender and Daniel G. Fuller

M. LiClar Publishing Co., LLC
Monroe City, MO

All rights reserved, including the right to reproduce this book or portions thereof in any form whatsoever.

ISBN: 0997024720
ISBN-13: 978-0-9970247-2-2

Scripture quotations are from the ESV® Bible (The Holy Bible, English Standard Version®), copyright © 2001 by Crossway, a publishing ministry of Good News Publishers. Used by permission. All rights reserved.

Contents

Introduction 5
Chapter 1: Foundations for the Feasts 16
Chapter 2: The Feast of Passover 37
Chapter 3: The Feast of Unleavened Bread 58
Chapter 4: The Feast of Firstfruits 74
Chapter 5: The Feast of Weeks or Pentecost 84
Chapter 6: The Events of Unleavened Bread 101
   Excursus: Where did the Old Testament Saints go at Death? 113
Chapter 7: The Feast of Trumpets 133
Chapter 8: The Day of Atonement 154
Chapter 9: The Feast of Tabernacles 168
Chapter 10: Already and Not Yet 183
Chapter 11: The Three Harvests 199
Chapter 12: The Divine Plan 213
Appendix: Tables of Sacrifices 219

Introduction

Years ago I visited South Africa and happened to be there during an important rugby game. This was just coincidental since I was totally ignorant of, and indifferent to, the sport. One person tried to make me understand the magnitude of this game by saying it was like the South African Super Bowl. I must say the rabid devotion I witnessed for the teams involved, the intensity of interest in the play on the field, and the exuberance or disappointment of the fans, depending on which team scored, mirrored what happens in front of American televisions during football games. Yet I was passive in all of this excitement. I didn't understand what was happening on the field and I had no attachment or loyalty to either team.

Contrast my boredom with the rugby game to when the Cardinals are playing in the World Series. In that context I am highly interested in the play on the field, committed to a desired outcome, and jubilant or crushed, depending on the final score. Yet my South African friend would probably sit passively, indifferent to the teams playing and the tremendous skill displayed. Maybe he would be curious about the rules of the game and would ask for an explanation of what was happening, but he would probably get bored at the snail's pace of baseball (according to critics).

If we step back from our favorite sports for a moment and look at them objectively, it really is rather silly what we get so worked up about. Consider the randomness and downright foolishness of sport:

- One player stands on a hill and throws a ball at his opponent who protects himself with a stick. If he successfully swats the ball away from himself he runs in a counterclockwise direction around a square that is called a diamond. But before running he drops his stick instead of keeping it with him to defend against the nine players on the other team who are still coming after him with that ball. Nine against one and he doesn't even get to keep his stick. How is that fair?

- Two sets of eleven players line up on opposite sides of an oblong piece of inflated leather. At one player's signal they all smash into each other, desperately going after the thing that is called a ball but does not share the spherical shape of every other ball known to mankind. Then they stop, line up, and do it again, all in an effort to carry the leather thing, that is referred to as pigskin, across a line to score six points. Then they will kick it between two tall poles. Oddly, sometimes when it is kicked between the poles it scores one point and other times it scores three.

- Suspended ten feet high at opposite ends of a wooden floor are two circular hoops attached to glass panels. A team of five works together to throw a large ball through one of the hoops while being opposed by another team trying to throw that ball through the hoop at the other end of the floor. When a player is in possession of the ball he may only move his feet while bouncing (dribbling) the ball, and he must dribble it with only one hand at a time. Once he stops bouncing the ball he may not bounce it again but must either throw it to a teammate or try to make it go through the hoop from the top, not from underneath.

And that is just a few of our major sports. The goals and rules of many of the more obscure Olympic and X-Game sports can get even more bizarre. They are like activities bored adolescents invent with whatever happens to be on hand—let's see if you can ride your skateboard off the roof while dodging these balls I will throw at you, shoot an arrow to hit a target on the tree and land in the pool. Oh yeah, if you add a 360 degree turn you score extra points.

Sports rules are really rather random when we think about them. And it is really rather comical that being the best at these strange activities is so important to us. Silly games have become multi-billion dollar industries heaping adulation on the gifted few who excel at doing basically irrelevant things.

We might assume that the feasts and sacrifices found in the Old Testament are also just made up oddities. Many a soul who has committed to reading through the Bible has struggled and bogged down in the book of Leviticus trying to slog through all the tedious regulations for proper sacrifices on specific feast days. These rules seem just as random and irrational as many competitive sports. Consider just a few examples of God's unusual requirements:

- The Israelites had to kill a lamb in the evening of the 14th day of the first month, then cook and eat it all that night, leaving no leftovers.

- On another day the Hebrews had to bake a couple of loaves of bread and wave them in the air before God.

Is that because the bread was hot and they were trying to cool them down, or were they spreading the fresh-baked smell?

- On the Day of Atonement God's people had to bring two goats. They had to do something like rolling dice to decide which one they would kill and which one they would send to get lost in the desert.

Did God randomly make up these rules just to test if his people would follow them? Are these strange rules the kind of "sport" God likes to watch?

The Bible is God's revelation of himself to man. If the rules for the feasts and their sacrifices are simply random, what would that say about God? We would have to conclude that God is random and nonsensical. Yet this would not fit with what we observe about God in the natural world. God's creation is incredibly complex with an almost infinite number of variables all coalescing together to make life possible. From the clockwork precision of galaxies spinning in the cosmos to the delicate intricacy of each unique snowflake, the universe is highly ordered and expertly assembled. Random and nonsensical is not part of God's creation, nor is it part of his character.

Instead, our confusion over the reasons for the feasts is like a teenager's assessment of her mother's rules: they are unnecessary and ridiculous. But as that teenager grows into adulthood and has her own child she will gain perspective and learn that her mother had very good reasons for the rules she imposed. She comes to appreciate her mother's wisdom as she gains an understanding of the benefits of those rules.

Likewise, God's regulations about the feasts appear arbitrary. But as we watch history unfold and as we comprehend more of his Word, we gain perspective. We see that God's specifications for observing the feasts all have a purpose.

Many churches have hosted *Christ in the Passover* events. These special worship services make explicit the connections between the observance of the Jewish Passover meal and the crucifixion of Christ. The New Testament leaves no doubt that this feast foreshadowed the death of Jesus, the ultimate Passover Lamb.

This book is built on the belief that not only the Passover, but all the feasts God commanded the Israelites to observe were meant to prophesy of the future. God obviously designed the Passover to picture Jesus' death on the cross. The other feasts also predict other aspects of God's plan.

Jesus said that not even the slightest bit of the Law would fail to be fulfilled (Matthew 5:18) and that he came to fulfill that Law. If Jesus came to accomplish every bit of the Old Testament Scriptures, then we should expect that the details God insisted the Israelites observe in the feasts were not random. These strange requirements were especially commanded to illustrate in advance what the Messiah would do.

Therefore, there are at least three basic reasons for the feasts God established in Israel:

1. The feasts proclaim God's blessing of the nations

2. The feasts picture God's salvation in full

3. The feasts prophesy God's redemptive program

The Feasts Proclaim God's Blessing

God promised to bless all the peoples on earth through Abraham (Genesis 12:3). Then he called the Israelites, Abraham's descendants, to be a kingdom of priests (Exodus 19:6). The observance of the feasts was a large part of the Jews' priestly duty. By carrying out God's instructions in celebrating the festivals, Israel was presenting to the world his plan for blessing all nations.

God did not choose Israel as his special people so that he could bless them and exclude all the other nations. He chose Israel to be the medium for communicating his blessings *to* all the other nations. When God brought the Hebrews out of slavery he did it in part to let the Egyptians know that he is the Lord (Exodus 7:5). Later, when the Israelites sinned in worshiping the golden calf at the foot of Mount Sinai, Moses interceded for them to turn away the Lord's wrath. He reasoned that destroying these rebellious people would reflect poorly on God. The Egyptians would conclude that God simply brought them out into the desert with the evil intent to kill them (Exodus 32:12). Moses understood that God chose to reveal himself to the world through Israel.

Often my parents and Sunday school teachers impressed upon me the idea that the world is watching. Other kids at school and in the neighborhood knew I went to church and was a Christian. If I acted contrary to my Christian belief they would recognize it. One of the reasons I was encouraged to do the right thing was to live as a good representative of Christ. The Jewish nation had the same responsibility.

So when Israel's neighbors watched them take off every seventh day they probably thought it strange. But the surrounding peoples must have really been baffled when the Jews would leave everything they owned and travel to Jerusalem three times a year. And they would do this at some of the peak harvesting times. Seeing the Israelite nation's strange behavior must have been just as perplexing for the gentile countries as the rugby game was to me.

While the regulations for the Jewish feasts were puzzling to Israel's neighbors, we should question them, too. And just like those ancient peoples, if we are willing to investigate what the Lord required we will see the blessings of a gracious God reaching out to an oppressed and rebellious people. And we will learn that those blessings are available to anyone who will turn toward that God in faith.

In the feasts, Israel was really putting on a play for the nations. They were acting out the story of what God would do to bring blessing to all people. They were a nation of priests receiving the message from God and presenting the greatest story ever told. They were the liaison communicating God's plan to the rest of mankind.

Today the church is likewise called to represent our Lord to a watching world. We must let our light shine for the world to see that they might praise our Father in heaven (Matthew 5:16). They are to know that we are Christians by our love of one another (John 13:35). Christian marriage is meant to display the love relationship between Christ and his church (Ephesians 5:31-32). God chooses to reveal himself to the world through his people. He does it today just as he has done throughout history. In the same way, the Jewish feasts were meant to show the true God for all to see.

After his resurrection Jesus walked along a road with two of his disciples, but they didn't recognize him. As they talked, Jesus explained the Old Testament Scriptures to them, showing them all the things that were written about himself. On that walk Jesus probably explained many things about the feasts that were fulfilled by his death and resurrection. The New Testament explicitly tells us that Passover and the Day of Atonement were prophesying about Jesus. It is reasonable to assume that all the feasts somehow point to Christ and we will see that they do. As Israel rehearsed these festivals year after year they were picturing what their Messiah would one day accomplish.

The Feasts Picture God's Salvation

We tend to cheapen salvation into a simple guarantee of eternal life for those who believe. We encourage people to trust in Jesus as Savior so they will go to heaven when they die. But that is only part of what God is doing in salvation. The feasts illustrate the depth and breadth of God's plan of redemption.

The Bible begins with creation and ends with a new creation. God is not simply interested in saving a few souls out of the world and scrapping everything else. He is working to bring his entire rebellious creation back into harmony with himself. He is accomplishing the most extreme makeover ever attempted. He does not plan to destroy the world, but to redeem it and remake it into a perfect haven as it was in the beginning. The feasts outline his plan from the ultimate sacrifice offered on the cross to the final consummation where everything in all creation is made new.

An understanding of the feasts helps us to see the scope of God's plan. The Christian needs to realize that salvation is not just insurance that will pay out once this life is over. Instead, we are the beginning of God's massive renovation. We are the new creation in Christ (2 Corinthians 5:17) that heralds the coming completion of God's work, the new heaven and the new earth. By studying the feasts we gain a deeper comprehension of our salvation and how we fit into God's grand plan for his creation.

The Feasts Prophesy God's Plan of Redemption

The New Testament draws direct lines from Passover, Firstfruits, Pentecost, and the Day of Atonement to the ministry of Christ. We can be very certain that these feasts were meant to picture Christ's work in advance. Many commentators have recognized the prophetic significance of the other feasts as well. But most have begun with their theories and theologies about the future and have placed the feasts on top of that. They have tried to use the feasts to bolster their particular interpretations. They have approached the feasts backwards.

Instead, God gave the feasts first to outline his redemptive program. For about 1,400 years God's people celebrated these annual illustrations that showed what Christ would do. God gave us this outline in the Old Testament and we see it being played out in history with the coming of the Messiah.

The feasts tell us not only what Christ has done but also what he will do. Many people are confused by biblical prophecies about the end times. There are a bewildering number of competing interpretations, so much so that many Christians have given up any hope of understanding any of it. They just trust that God will work it all out as he sees best.

But if we are not meant to understand anything about the end times, why did God write about it in the Scriptures? The book of Revelation promises blessing to the one who reads and understands. We miss out on this blessing and we ignore large portions of what God chose to reveal to us in his Word if we just throw up our hands in surrender, thinking we will never comprehend future prophecies.

The feasts offer us a template for organizing biblical prophecies. God has provided an outline of his plan of redemption in the Old Testament festivals. And this outline encompasses his entire program that culminates in a new heaven and a new earth. Armed with an understanding of the feasts, we will be able to tackle prophetic texts that previously seemed indecipherable. We will also find that eschatology, the study of last things or the end times, is not just an optional add on to our faith. It is integral to God's plan of redemption for his fallen world.

As we study, we will also find that the feasts not only have application for prophetic texts but for other biblical passages as well. Some seemingly obscure and random verses will suddenly make perfect sense in the light of God's overall plan. In fact, the feasts will demonstrate for us the incredible unity of all of the Scriptures. Just as all the facets of God's creation work together to keep the world going, all the details of his Word fit together into his grand plan.

So instead of beginning with a theory or interpretation of the end times, we need to learn from the feasts first and discern what they teach and the prophetic pattern they establish. Then we will have a basis for interpreting other prophetic texts as well. We must start with the feasts and move to the future, not vice versa. And that is what we will do in this book. We will study the seven biblical feasts in Leviticus 23 where we will find the outline for God's plan of redemption throughout the ages.

Chapter 1: Foundations for the Feasts

> *The LORD spoke to Moses, saying, "Speak to the people of Israel and say to them, These are the appointed feasts of the LORD that you shall proclaim as holy convocations; they are my appointed feasts. Six days shall work be done, but on the seventh day is a Sabbath of solemn rest, a holy convocation. You shall do no work. It is a Sabbath to the LORD in all your dwelling places."*
> **Leviticus 23:1-3**

In Leviticus 23 God outlined the special feasts that his people, Israel, were to observe in worship. The seven feasts are:

1. The Feast of Passover

2. The Feast of Unleavened Bread

3. The Feast of Firstfruits

4. The Feast of Weeks (Pentecost)

5. The Feast of Trumpets (Rosh Hashanah)

6. The Day of Atonement (Yom Kippur)

7. The Feast of Tabernacles (Booths)

The apostle Paul tells us that these feasts, along with the new moon (celebration of the first day of each month) and the Sabbath, are all a shadow of things to come.

Therefore let no one pass judgment on you in questions of food and drink, or with regard to a festival or a new moon or a Sabbath. These are a shadow of the things to come, but the substance belongs to Christ.

Colossians 2:16-17

The seven feasts of Leviticus 23 foreshadow the realities that are realized in Christ. But before God laid out the seven feasts, he spoke of the weekly feast day. The Sabbath is the one feast and the one formal act of worship that God included in the Ten Commandments.

The Sabbath

In Exodus 20, the fourth commandment is to honor the Sabbath day. God commands Moses and the Israelites to observe the Sabbath because God created the world in six days and then rested on the seventh. So from creation there is something fundamental about a seven day week, we can't escape it. Various governments and peoples have tried to alter this pattern, but without success.

The atheistic Soviet Union did not like the association of the seven day week with religious significance. They also thought they could increase productivity by changing the length of a week. The Soviets experimented with a five day and also a six day week. But they couldn't make it work and ultimately returned to the seven day week.[1] There is just something fundamental about the seven day week. But why is that? What establishes a week?

---

[1] Rosenberg, Jennifer. "Soviets Change the Calendar." About.com Education. 18 Nov. 2015. Web. 27 Mar. 2016.

- A day is 24 hours because that is the length of time for the earth to rotate on its axis once.
- A month is approximately 30 days because the moon passes through all its phases in that time.
- A year is 365¼ days because that is how long it takes for the earth to orbit the sun.

But what establishes a week? There are no astronomical movements that identify a week.

It has been suggested that the lunar cycle was divided into four so that a week would represent the length of time from one phase of the moon to the next. But this does not really fit. And why was it divided into four and not two? It would have been easier to distinguish the 14 day week as the moon waxes from new to full, and then a waning 14 day week as it returns to a new moon. It is also curious that the seven day week came about in contrast to other astronomical calculations of time that are based on units of 12 (hours of daytime and nighttime, months in a year) and 60 (seconds in a minute, minutes in an hour). Seven does not fit neatly into these number patterns. There just isn't a good natural answer as to why a week is seven days.

The best reason for a week being seven days is because God ordained it. Sabbath observance just follows this pattern that was established at the very beginning.

In Deuteronomy 5 Moses reminds the Israelites of the Ten Commandments and gives another reason for Sabbath observance. This time the reason is based on God's deliverance of the Hebrews from Egyptian slavery. Because the Jews are no longer slaves they have the freedom to take a day off every week. The slave enjoyed no such luxury but was subject to forced labor every day. The Sabbath is a weekly reminder that God's people are free.

The Sabbath becomes the great equalizer. God leaves no room for the landholder to take a rest while still having his employees out working in the fields. The Scripture is quite clear that everyone gets to enjoy the day off, not just those in power. Men and women, slave and free, young and old, native and foreigner alike are relieved from duties on the Sabbath.

Sabbath observance also straightens our priorities. It is a Sabbath *to the Lord.* The Sabbath is a time for stepping back from our daily tasks and reorienting ourselves toward God. First of all, we do this out of obedience. God commands it, so that is enough.

We also observe the Sabbath out of trust in the Lord. We believe that God will provide even when we rest a day. God will make what we can accomplish in six days enough to carry us through seven. Now this might not seem like much, but in a highly competitive society, we believe we can't stay in the race when one day out of seven we sit out. As we know, the hare was very fast, but when he stopped to take a nap the plodding tortoise passed him and won the race.

The step of faith becomes even larger when the Sabbath principle is extended. God told his people not only to observe a weekly Sabbath, but to observe a Sabbath month each year and a Sabbath year every seven.

The final three feasts occurred in the seventh month of the year. The month began with a special Sabbath celebration on the Feast of Trumpets and included another extra Sabbath for the Day of Atonement and two more Sabbath observances to open and close the Feast of Booths or Tabernacles. Combine these with the regular weekly Sabbaths and the seventh month holds at least eight days of rest, more than any other month in the year. Thus it truly is a Sabbath month. And to make it more challenging, all these extra Sabbaths happen during harvest time when it is imperative to get the crops in before they are stolen by either two-footed or four-footed thieves, or before they rot on the vine.

But a Sabbath month is nothing compared to the leap of faith in taking the Sabbatical year. Every seventh year the Israelites were to refrain from plowing their fields and planting their crops. They were to take the year off and simply eat what grew wild. Can you imagine being a farmer and leaving your fields fallow for an entire year, simply trusting that the crop of the sixth year will be enough to see you and your family through to the harvest of the eighth year? Observing the Sabbath re-orders our priorities and stretches our faith as it demonstrates in very concrete terms that we are not in control, God is.

The Sabbaths

While the Sabbath was the seventh day, it does not simply equal what we call Saturday. Sabbath is more than just a particular day of the week. Leviticus 23 tells us that the seventh day Sabbath is not the end, it is just the beginning. There are other Sabbaths, other special days for the Israelites to rest from their labors, offer sacrifices to God, and celebrate the blessings of being his people.

Because of the Sabbath, **seven** becomes an important number God chooses to use. And the seven Jewish feasts are a prime example. God must be saying something extremely important in the seven feasts to require that they be repeated year after year exactly according to his instructions. For about 1,400 years God's people rehearsed the story of the feasts until finally, in the fullness of time, God sent his Son to be **the** Passover Lamb. God firmly established his design in these festivals so that when the time came we could understand and recognize what he was doing to save us. The feasts are not peripheral material in the Scriptures. They are a basic and essential picture of God's plan for redeeming his fallen world.

Just as God finished creating the world in seven days, he will complete redeeming the world through what he pictures in seven feasts. The extension of the Sabbath principle onto the feasts is evident in that the seventh feast is the most joyous celebration of all. The Feast of Tabernacles, the seventh feast, closes out the year of festivals with an exuberant display of gratitude for all God's wonderful gifts. The Feast of Tabernacles is like the Sabbath of feasts, if you will.

With God's eternal purpose in mind, we must not assume that any of the details God chose to include in the feasts is random. Everything has its purpose.

For example, consider the placement of the feasts in the year. Who in their right mind would stack a bunch of holidays all together in a row? Why not spread them out through the year and pace ourselves? Yet that is what we have done with the end of our year. Thanksgiving, Christmas, and the New Year have become over a month long period we collectively refer to as "the holidays." We get stressed out every year as we stuff ourselves with turkey and then plunge into a mad frenzy of buying gifts, decorating our houses, attending extra worship services, going to concerts, and having parties at home, school, and work. We do this at a time when students are taking final exams, the government is collecting year end taxes and requiring paperwork for the new year, and the weather is very likely to be terrible for at least a few of those days causing cancellations, postponements, and rescheduling. It's no wonder the holidays are an extra stressful time of year.

Of course, no one had a grand plan that set up the craziness of December. The holiday season just developed over the years and this is what we are stuck with. But God did have a grand plan. He could see into the future and anticipate how things would work out. So why did he create the same kind of logjam that we foolish Americans foisted upon ourselves?

God set up seven important feasts and he crammed them all into basically two short seasons. The first three feasts all happen in the first month of the year within just a few days of each other. The last three feasts are in the seventh month from the 1st through the 22nd. Only Pentecost falls outside of these two months, but it is just 50 days after Firstfruits. So God packed all seven feasts into the spring and one month in the fall.

Distribution of the Feasts on the Calendar

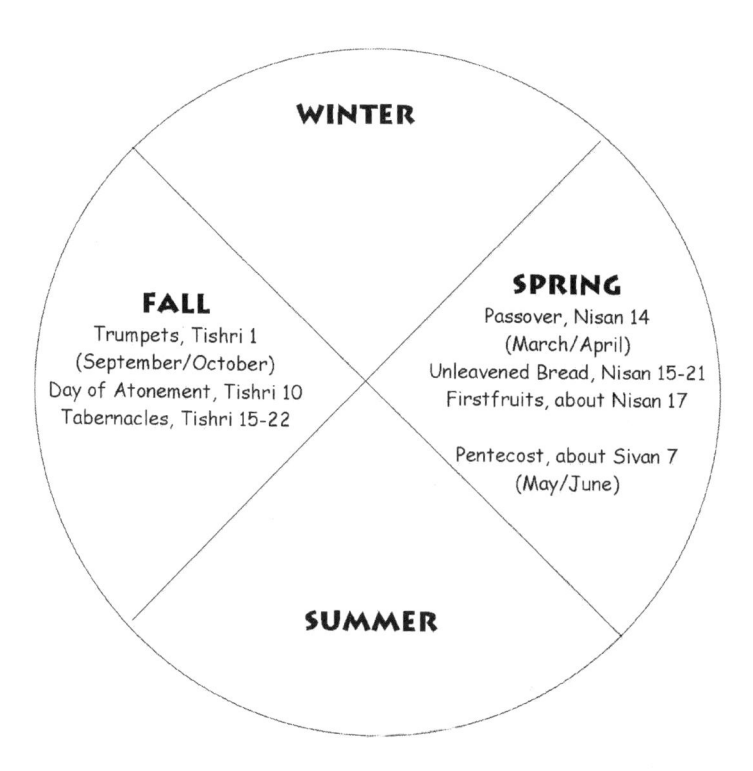

WINTER

FALL
Trumpets, Tishri 1
(September/October)
Day of Atonement, Tishri 10
Tabernacles, Tishri 15-22

SPRING
Passover, Nisan 14
(March/April)
Unleavened Bread, Nisan 15-21
Firstfruits, about Nisan 17

Pentecost, about Sivan 7
(May/June)

SUMMER

Why didn't God spread out the feasts? In the weekly Sabbath the Lord teaches us the wisdom of pacing ourselves. A rhythm of work and rest interspersed consistently is more productive and healthier than a long period of constant struggle followed by a crash into exhaustion. Yet God purposefully placed all of his feasts within two small time periods in the year.

This was not a mistake. God did it for a reason. We must pay attention to understand what it tells us about God's redemptive program.

The Sacrifices

Another aspect of the feasts that we must not neglect is the sacrifices. Particular sacrifices were required on particular days. And the type and number of sacrifices varied according to the feast being observed. God is saying something through the sacrifices also.

Earlier we noted how confusing reading through the Old Testament can be. Possibly the most bewildering thing to our modern sensibilities is the variety of sacrifices. The specific occasion for sacrifice determined whether the offering was animal or vegetable, what quantity was required, and what ritual was performed. The rules for each sacrifice can sound like a foreign language to 21st century people who are completely removed from a sacrificial culture.

But we don't need to feel overwhelmed trying to understand the sacrifices. Here is a basic outline of the hierarchy of sacrifices.

The Hierarchy of Sacrifice

- Type of animal from greater to lesser: 1) Herd (cattle), 2) Flock (sheep and goats), 3) Birds

- Gender of animal from greater to lesser: 1) Male, 2) Female

- Person offering the sacrifice from greater to lesser: 1) Priest or Whole Community, 2) Leader of Community, 3) Individual Member of Community

God made a covenant with Abram and told him to sacrifice a heifer, goat, ram, dove and pigeon (Genesis 15:9). In this sacrifice we see the three classes of animals that can be offered to God: 1) sacrifices from the herd (cattle), 2) sacrifices from the flock (sheep and goats), and 3) sacrifices of birds. This is also in order of the hierarchy of acceptable animals for sacrifice. A sacrifice from the herd was most valuable followed by the flock and then the birds.

Beyond the type of animal sacrificed, we see that males were more valuable than females. A female animal was acceptable for some instances, but often a male was required due to the gravity of an occasion. And then multiplying the number of animals offered constituted a greater sacrifice. Basically the rule of thumb is the more important the offering, or the greater the sin being atoned for, the greater the sacrifice.

Thus we see that the daily offering was two male lambs, each a year old and without blemish, but on the weekly Sabbath this is doubled to four lambs (Numbers 28:9-10). The sacrifice is increased beyond the normal on the special day of the week, the Sabbath. Also, when an ordinary member of the community sinned his offering was a female lamb or goat, but when a priest sinned he had to offer a bull (Leviticus 4:3). The significance of the priest's position, as one who mediated between God and man, required that he bring a greater sacrifice for his transgressions. The New Testament echoes this principle with the heightened responsibility and stricter judgment of those in leadership (James 3:1).

Considering the hierarchy of sacrifice, it is strange that the crucifixion of Christ is pictured by a lamb at Passover and a goat on the Day of Atonement. These two sacrifices that most particularly represent the incomprehensible work of Christ come from the second, not the highest level of animal sacrifice. Of course, every type of animal offered ultimately foreshadowed Christ since his death put an end to all sacrifice. All of those animals had only been shadows of what Jesus would do once for all. But Passover and the Day of Atonement are the two feasts that very emphatically declared what Christ would do on the cross. Why wouldn't the death of the Son of God warrant the most costly sacrifice to illustrate it?

The reason these sacrifices come from the second class of animals is found in the nature of the sacrificial animal. A bull is a strong, intimidating creature. By contrast a lamb is meek and mild. And this is the way Jesus came to give himself up for us. Not as a powerful bull, but as a lamb led to the slaughter. Not as a snorting, fearsome behemoth striking terror in the hearts of its captors, but as a sheep silent before the shearers (Isaiah 53:7).

While a bull was a very valuable animal, it was certainly not one you would take in as the family pet. But you could get very attached to a lamb. Although it is just a parable, there is truth in Nathan's story of the man who treated a lamb like his own daughter (2 Samuel 12:3). The lamb shared his food, drank from his cup, and slept in his arms. So it is a powerful image when God likens the death of his Son with the sacrifice of a lamb. God comes to us in the flesh, not as someone to be feared, but as our meek and gentle friend. And then he lays down his life for us.

Three Types of Sacrifices

The other fact to keep in mind with the animal sacrifices is that there are really just three types: 1) the sin offering, 2) the burnt offering, and 3) the fellowship offering. Each of these offerings has a distinct emphasis that pictures a different aspect of God's salvation.[2]

The differences in the three basic types of offerings is summarized in the following table:

Type of Sacrifice	Dominant Characteristic	Aspect of Salvation Pictured
Sin Offering	Sprinkling of blood	Justification
Burnt Offering	Complete burning	Sanctification
Fellowship Offering	Eating meal	Glorification

In the **sin offering** the dominant characteristic is the sprinkling of blood. The throat of the animal was slit and the blood was drained out into a bowl. That blood was then sprinkled on either people or objects to cleanse them from sin, depending on what particular sacrifice was being made. Hebrews 9:22 says "without the shedding of blood there is no forgiveness of sins." Once the blood was sprinkled, portions of the sin offering were burnt on the altar while other portions became the property of the priests who ate the meat. The sin of the person offering the sacrifice was covered by the blood. So the sin offering primarily represents

---

[2] J.H. Kurtz, *Offerings, Sacrifices and Worship in the Old Testament,* Hendrickson Publishers, Inc., 1998, p. 64.

justification. *Justification* is the aspect of our salvation where God, the Judge, accepts the sacrificial substitute as payment for the crime and declares the person not guilty.

The guilt offering or trespass offering is a special type of sin offering for offenses committed against the Lord's holy things (Leviticus 5:15). A person might sin against the Lord's holy things by, for instance, failing to fulfill a vow made to the Lord or by participating in worship after becoming unclean through contact with a dead body. Such a person would have to bring a guilt offering, which is a sin offering plus making restitution to the Lord for what he failed to do (Leviticus 5:16).

Sanctified means "made holy" or "totally set apart for God's use." *Sanctification* is pictured in the burnt offering. **The burnt offering or whole burnt offering** means exactly what the name suggests. The sacrifice was placed on the altar and completely consumed in the fire. This is the special characteristic of the offering, that the whole animal was given to God and nothing was left over for anyone else. The burnt offering illustrates our sanctification, being set apart completely to the Lord, as the sacrifice was wholly given to God.

When the **fellowship or peace offering** was brought, a portion was burned on the altar and another portion was cooked and eaten by the person offering the sacrifice. Symbolically the worshiper entered into fellowship with God by sharing a meal. This anticipates our *glorification*, the ultimate goal of our salvation when our faith becomes sight and we dwell in the presence of the Lord forever.

Each feast called for different offerings, usually sacrifices from two or three of these categories. But one sacrifice takes precedence in each feast. Paying attention to the type of sacrifice that is emphasized gives insight into what God was communicating in the celebration of the festival and what event it was prophesying.

The Animals Required for Sacrifice

Previously we noted the hierarchy of sacrificial animals, how a sacrifice from the herd (cattle) was the most costly, followed by sacrifices from the flock (sheep and goats) and then birds. But what is the significance of the animal specified for each occasion? If God very particularly commanded that certain animals be offered at certain times, then there is probably a reason for it. And that reason illustrates something about God's plan.

Numbers 28 and 29 are companion chapters to Leviticus 23. While the Leviticus passage outlines the seven feasts, Numbers details the offerings prescribed for each day. The most basic sacrifice is the daily burnt offering of two lambs, each a year old. One lamb was offered in the morning and the other at twilight (Numbers 28:3-4) every day of the year. This was a continual burnt offering as the lamb from the morning would burn throughout the day and the one offered in the evening would burn all night. This constant burning of the lambs represented the fact that Israel was forever set apart to be God's holy people.

But why was the daily sacrifice required to be a lamb? Considering precedent, the sacrifice of a lamb immediately calls to mind Passover. That is the definitive moment that transformed the Hebrews from a bunch of slaves into a nation. The blood of the Passover lambs spared the firstborn sons and freed God's people from slavery. But not only did God command the lambs be slain in place of the firstborn at that first Passover, every subsequent generation of firstborn Israelites was also redeemed with the offer of a lamb (Exodus 13:15). The lamb sacrifice was a constant reminder of the Passover.

So each time a lamb was offered it recalled Passover. The daily sacrifice of two lambs burning on the altar every day and every night were in remembrance of the Passover lambs that saved the children of Israel from death and won them freedom. And those lambs also looked forward to the one Lamb that would die to save us all from death and give us true freedom.

As mentioned before, the sacrifice on the Sabbath was double the daily sacrifice. Along with the normal two lambs offered each day, another two lambs were sacrificed on the seventh day of the week, the day of rest. This establishes a pattern that is followed in the seventh month of the year, the Sabbath month, where some sacrifices are doubled during the Feast of Tabernacles. We will study those sacrifices in a later chapter.

After Numbers 28 specifies the daily and Sabbath offerings it goes on to list the monthly offering. The new moon signaled the beginning of a new month. Israel was to offer two bulls, one ram, and seven lambs as a burnt offering along with one goat as a sin offering on the first day of each month. Twelve times a year this combination of animals was offered up. Not only that, this new moon collection of offerings sets a standard that is duplicated in two feasts (Unleavened Bread and Pentecost) and is very slightly modified in three others (Trumpets, Day of Atonement, and Tabernacles). So this grouping of sacrifices seems very important. But what is the significance of these types and numbers of sacrificial animals?

Again, considering precedent, when we hear of one ram being offered the story of the sacrifice of Isaac should leap into our minds (Genesis 22). This is the first occasion in the Bible where a ram is particularly noted as being offered as a sacrifice. And this ram becomes an incredible picture of Christ's substitutionary atonement. The ram takes the place of Isaac on the altar just as Jesus takes our place on the cross. Each month God's people would offer a ram picturing the sacrifice of their coming Savior.

We might wonder about what distinguished a ram from a male lamb. The difference between a ram and a lamb was maturity. The Hebrew word translated "ram" is literally "strength." So the ram was full grown, probably three years old, as compared to the one year old lambs.

Considering the bull, the first time the Bible specifies that a bull was sacrificed is in the ordination of Aaron and his sons as priests (Exodus 29:10; Leviticus 8:14). This, then, becomes the standard for any priest who sins, he must offer a bull for a sin offering (Leviticus 4:3). A bull is also required to atone for a sin committed by the whole congregation of Israel (Leviticus 4:14). The entire nation was a kingdom of priests so the bull is a fitting sacrifice as it follows the pattern set for the priests. Since the monthly sacrifice called for two bulls to be offered, they seem to represent the priests and the priestly nation, respectively.

This brings us to the seven lambs in the monthly offering. The lamb reminds us of Passover, but why seven? Seven is the number of creation and completion, but it is also the number of the Gentile church. Consider these biblical instances where seven very pointedly attaches to the nations other than Israel, or God's people from those nations, the church, just as the number twelve connects to Israel.

- Within the tabernacle was a seven-branched lampstand that seems to represent the Gentile church. In John's vision in Revelation 1, Christ appears among seven lampstands that are identified as seven churches. These seven local Gentile churches of Asia Minor are representative of God's people, the church as a whole, which is predominantly Gentile. Therefore, the seven-branched lampstand is representative of the church just as the twelve unleavened loaves on the table in the tabernacle represented the tribes of Israel. So within the tabernacle are represented God's people, Israel and the church.

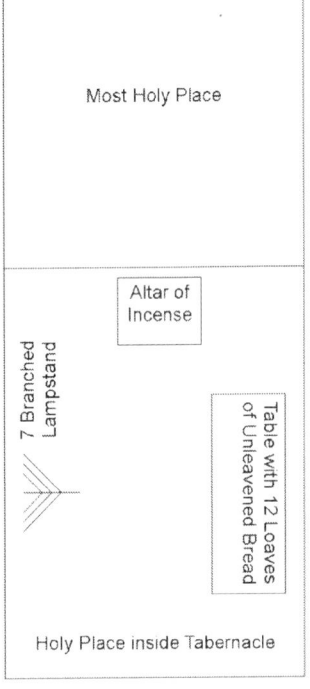

- On two different occasions Jesus multiplied loaves and fishes to feed large crowds. Jesus fed the 5,000 in the largely Jewish vicinity of Bethsaida (Luke 9:10).

He later fed 4,000 in the predominantly Gentile region of the Decapolis (Mark 7:31). The disciples collected twelve baskets full of leftovers in the Jewish area and seven baskets in the Gentile area. So again, seven attaches to the Gentile church just as twelve attaches to Israel.

- The early church was experiencing growing pains as a cultural dispute broke out (Acts 6). While all the believers shared a Jewish background, some were Hebraic and others Grecian. The Hebraic believers followed traditional Jewish culture more closely, while the Grecian Jews had assimilated into the Hellenistic way of doing things, adopting some of the living practices of the Greeks. To solve the problem, the church appointed seven men to serve the needs of the Grecian widows at the center of the controversy.

Immediately after the ordination of the seven the church starts growing among Gentiles. The stoning of one of the seven, Stephen, disperses the church into non-Jewish areas where they begin to see Gentile converts. Philip, another of the seven, leads a great revival among the Samaritans. The infant Jewish church was led by twelve apostles while the Gentile church expanded from the seven. Thus twelve is more typically a Jewish number and seven is the number of the Gentile church.

The monthly offering of seven lambs, then, would picture the salvation of the Gentile church. Israel was saved and constituted as a nation by the sacrifice of the Passover lamb. The Gentiles are also saved by the Lamb, Jesus, and are made into a people, the people of God.

Therefore, within the monthly burnt offering of two bulls, one ram, and seven lambs we have a picture of Christ redeeming his people. In the ram we see Jesus giving himself on our behalf. His sacrifice consecrates, on the one hand, a nation of priests and a family of priests within that nation signified by the two bulls. But just as God promised that all nations would be blessed through Abraham (Genesis 12:3), Christ's sacrifice also consecrates a people from all nations, represented by the seven lambs.

Even the order in which this group of sacrifices is listed may be significant. While it is possible that the order simply follows the hierarchy of sacrificial animals, bulls from the herd before rams and lambs from the flock, there could be another reason. We previously noted how the two groups of God's people were represented in the tabernacle. The table of twelve consecrated loaves pictured Israel and the seven branched lampstand represented the church. These were placed opposite each other, as if one were on God's right hand and the other on his left. In the monthly offering, the ram, picturing Christ dying for us as substitute, is listed between the other sacrifices, the two bulls representing Israel and the seven lambs representing the church. So Christ is in the middle with his people from Israel on one hand and his people from the Gentile nations on the other.

Here is the picture we get from the monthly sacrifice.

The Monthly Burnt Offering

Sacrificial Animals	2 Bulls	1 Ram	7 Lambs
What They Represent	Israel (Priests + Nation)	Christ our Substitute	Gentile Church

The monthly sacrifice also featured a sin offering of one goat along with the burnt offerings. It is on the Day of Atonement where a goat takes center stage and sets the precedent for the meaning of this offering. The sprinkling of the goat's blood provided atonement, or covering, for sin. This prophesied the shedding of Christ's blood that washes us from our sins and allows us fellowship with God. The ram emphasized substitution as Christ offered himself on our behalf. Now the goat emphasizes atonement as Jesus' blood offers us entrance into the presence of a holy God.

The Lord laid out his plan of atonement in the sacrifices he required of the Israelites. On the first of each month the priests would offer these sacrifices that tell the story of Christ's death on behalf of his people, both Jew and Gentile, that brings us into fellowship with a holy God.

The Recipe

The book of Hebrews tells us that the Old Testament sacrificial system was a shadow of the realities to come (Hebrews 10:1). The former system is related to the new just as a recipe is related to the finished product. My wife uses a recipe for baking chocolate chip cookies. The recipe identifies the necessary ingredients—milk, eggs, flour, vanilla, chocolate chips, etc. It also specifies the amounts needed and gives instruction on the order of combining all of these items to reach the desired result. But while the recipe is very good and necessary, it is incomplete and unsatisfying. It is just words and pictures printed on paper. My boys and I can't eat it. Only when the recipe is followed and the delicious cookies are produced can we then enjoy them. The recipe is only a shadow of the reality of the cookies.

This is how the feasts relate to our salvation. Like the recipe, they outline everything that is needed and describe the order in which they must be combined to achieve the goal. Yet they are not the reality themselves. The feasts do not provide salvation for God's people.

But the feasts are the recipe that God uses. At just the right time the Lord set about following this recipe that he wrote down hundreds of years in advance. The New Testament explains to us, for instance, that Jesus is the Passover Lamb who takes away the sin of the world. God gave Passover to the Jews as the first ingredient to describe the salvation he would provide for the world. Therefore, we see in the feasts the recipe or shadow of God's plan of redemption that he began at the cross and will carry on to completion as he mixes in each of the seven ingredients. The feasts are the recipe for the future.

Chapter 2: The Feast of Passover

> *In the first month, on the fourteenth day of the month at twilight, is the LORD's Passover.*
>
> **Leviticus 23:5**

The celebration of Passover occurs in the spring. As Jewish families gather for a special meal, the youngest child is prompted to ask a series of four questions. The elder members answer these questions that recount the story of Israel's exodus from Egypt and explain the significance of the feast. This tradition originated from Scriptures like this one from Exodus:

> *And when your children say to you, 'What do you mean by this service?' you shall say, 'It is the sacrifice of the LORD's Passover, for he passed over the houses of the people of Israel in Egypt, when he struck the Egyptians but spared our houses.'*
>
> **Exodus 12:26-27**

Each year parents and grandparents retell the story of Passover, recalling the sacrificed lambs represented by a shank bone on the table, the Jewish slaves' hard labor signified by the dish of bitter herbs, and their quick flight into freedom in the desert that forced them to eat unleavened bread. As wide-eyed Jewish boys and girls take notice of all the special items on the table that night, they learn a lesson from each one. The Passover and all its unique components are meant to transport modern Jews back to the days of the exodus to remember the place from whence they came, and the God who performed his miracles on their behalf.

But the Passover does not only look backward to the deliverance of the Hebrews from slavery. It also looks forward to a greater deliverance that would be accomplished by "the Lamb of God who takes away the sin of the world" (John 1:29). Just as each element of the Passover meal helps to tell the story of the exodus, each detail of the feast also points us to Christ. God painted a picture in Passover that foretold how he would redeem humanity from slavery to sin by offering his Son as substitute. In Leviticus 23:5 we get a simple statement as to when Passover occurs. For a more detailed description of the celebration of Passover we need to turn to Exodus 12.

> *The LORD said to Moses and Aaron in the land of Egypt, "This month shall be for you the beginning of months. It shall be the first month of the year for you. Tell all the congregation of Israel that on the tenth day of this month every man shall take a lamb according to their fathers' houses, a lamb for a household. And if the household is too small for a lamb, then he and his nearest neighbor shall take according to the number of persons; according to what each can eat you shall make your count for the lamb. Your lamb shall be without blemish, a male a year old. You may take it from the sheep or from the goats, and you shall keep it until the fourteenth day of this month, when the whole assembly of the congregation of Israel shall kill their lambs at twilight.*
>
> *"Then they shall take some of the blood and put it on the two doorposts and the lintel of the houses in which they eat it. They shall eat the flesh that night, roasted on the fire; with unleavened bread and bitter herbs they shall eat it. Do not eat any of it raw or boiled in water, but*

roasted, its head with its legs and its inner parts. And you shall let none of it remain until the morning; anything that remains until the morning you shall burn. In this manner you shall eat it: with your belt fastened, your sandals on your feet, and your staff in your hand. And you shall eat it in haste. It is the LORD's Passover. For I will pass through the land of Egypt that night, and I will strike all the firstborn in the land of Egypt, both man and beast; and on all the gods of Egypt I will execute judgments: I am the LORD. The blood shall be a sign for you, on the houses where you are. And when I see the blood, I will pass over you, and no plague will befall you to destroy you, when I strike the land of Egypt."

Exodus 12:1-13

God gave Moses some very specific instructions in this passage. We will consider each of those requirements and their significance in both looking backward to the exodus and forward to the cross.

The First Month of the Year

God told Moses that this month in the spring would be their first month of the year. That is in contrast to the accepted contemporary calendar whose year began in the fall. The Jews maintained that new year, which came to be called *Rosh Hashanah*, for their civil year, but made this month in the spring the beginning of their religious year. This is Israel's first month of the year because it contains the defining event that delivers them from slavery and makes them a free people. It is only fitting that this should be the beginning of their year.

But the feast also anticipates that Jesus' death on the cross as THE Passover Lamb will be the defining event that delivers us from slavery to sin and makes us a free people. It is the beginning and defining event through which God saves his world.

The Passover Lamb

The lamb that was chosen had to be enough for those in the household, but not too much. If necessary, neighbors were to join together so that the amount of lamb would feed everyone and not leave too much uneaten, because those leftovers had to be burned the next morning.

It was important that the lamb be enough but not too much because the Passover was a one-time deliverance from slavery. There was also the very practical reason that the Jews fleeing the country did not need anything extra weighing them down on their journey.

So, just as the Passover was a one-time event that delivered Israel from Egypt, Christ died once for all. There is no need to repeat. Eating the lamb another day would have destroyed the imagery of Christ's once and for all sacrifice that was finished on the cross. And just as the Passover was for all Israelites, Christ is enough for us all. His death was sufficient for all our sins and was for all of us.

The chosen lambs were also to be year old males without defect. Israel had to offer to God their best, not leftovers. This fact pointed forward to Jesus, who was the Lamb of God without defect. He had no sin and was certified as pure, not only by God the Father but also by the Jewish leaders who could find no charge against him (except that he claimed to be the Son of God, which he really was). The Roman governor, Pontius Pilate, also could find no charge against him and was ready to let him go. He tried to sidestep responsibility by sending him to Herod but he, too, declined to level any charge against Jesus. Finally, it was only at the insistence of the crowd that Pilate chose to appease them by crucifying Jesus. So he was certified as without defect three times over: by the Father, the Jewish high council, and the ruling Romans.

The Blood Sprinkled

The Jews took another step of faith in placing the blood of the lamb on the tops and sides of their doors. This was a blatant statement that one believed that God was going to deliver them that night. The blood on the door tells us that the only entrance into the household of God is through the blood. As the door is the entryway into the home, Jesus is the Door, the entryway into the household of God (John 10:7-9).

God commanded that the blood be placed on both sides and the top of the doorway. Why was this necessary? Wouldn't a dab of blood anywhere on the door have been sufficient? Was the angel of the Lord nearsighted so that he needed a lot of blood to see it?

In the classic Charlton Heston movie, *The Ten Commandments*, the Israelites painted huge swaths of blood on their doors. But that is not accurate. The Hebrews did not have paint brushes that would soak up large amounts of blood and spread it evenly with a few strokes. They used branches of hyssop, a small plant standing from 12 to 24 inches tall. It has a woody stem from which grow several straight branches. Not an ideal paintbrush, hyssop would only hold a small amount of blood that could then be dabbed onto the door.

The King James translation that says "they shall take of the blood, and *strike* it on the two side posts and on the upper door post" (Exodus 12:7) probably accurately describes how the blood was applied. After a few strikes of the hyssop, there would be a splotch of blood on the door.

So the Hebrews would have ended up with a couple of spatters of blood on either side of the door and another one above the door. The blood on both sides of the door would naturally suggest a horizontal line. And the blood on the top of the door would eventually drip down on the threshold suggesting a vertical line. God drew a cross in blood nearly 1000 years before crucifixion was invented as a method of execution. He indicated the type of death his Son would suffer over 1400 years before the fact.

Branch of Hyssop

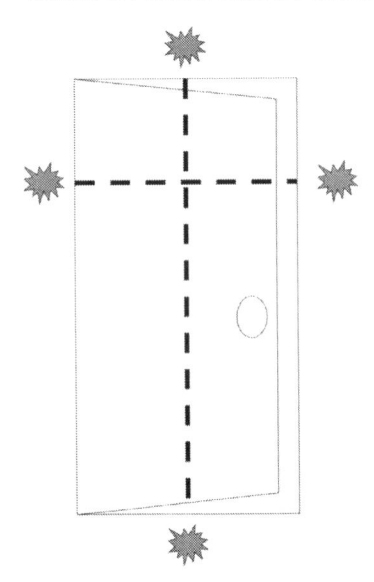

Blood on Door

The Unleavened Bread

The Jews had to hurriedly make their bread on that Passover day, there was no time to let the dough rise. They ate what they called the "bread of affliction" that was not soft and tasty but flat and crispy. Yet this bread was not a burden, but actually a sweet reminder of their deliverance. Here God establishes leaven or yeast as a symbol for sin. This remains consistent throughout Scripture as leaven always symbolizes sin in the Bible. The leaven was not only removed from the bread, but had to be completely expelled from the house. Christ was without sin and he cleanses us from all sin.

Some interpreters have debated whether leaven always represents sin. The regulations for the feasts of Passover and Unleavened Bread forbid leaven. Yet the Old Testament does not specify why leaven must be removed. Leviticus 2:11 lays down the rule that nothing leavened can be offered on the altar. Even though leavened items could be brought as offerings to the Lord, they were never burned on the altar. Still, the Hebrew Scriptures are silent on the reasons for these commands.

But where the Old Testament is ambiguous, vague, or silent, the New Testament is often clear. Jesus labeled the false teachings of the Pharisees and Sadducees as leaven (Matthew 16:12; Mark 8:15; Luke 12:1). Paul exhorted the Corinthians to purge out the leaven of sin represented by their approval of immorality (1 Corinthians 5:7-8). Paul illustrates his plea with the removal of leaven at Passover and Unleavened Bread, showing that he believes that the reason leaven was removed was because it represented sin. Both Jesus and Paul spoke of leaven as representing falsehood and sin.

Still, some commentators point to Jesus' parable of the leaven as an instance when leaven does not represent sin (Matthew 13:33; Luke 13:21). There Jesus compares the kingdom of God to a woman kneading leaven into her dough, leaven that eventually spreads throughout the whole lump. These interpreters see the leaven as a picture of Christ's kingdom that grows and permeates the world. But this interpretation is backwards. Several factors point us to understand that Jesus is saying that his kingdom will still include sin, and that sin will spread.

1. **It is a woman who mixes the leaven into the dough.** Throughout Matthew 13 Jesus gives parables of the kingdom. In each story, Christ is represented as a man who plants the seeds of the kingdom or searches for treasure. But in this one instance Jesus says it is a woman adding the leaven. Christ hints that the leaven is not a good thing since he is not the one adding it.

2. **The parable of the leaven is paired with the parable of the mustard seed.** There we see the great growth of the mustard tree, representing the kingdom, but also the birds roosting in its branches. Earlier in the 13th chapter of Matthew the parable of the sower featured birds that represented Satan. So just as the parable of the mustard seed has devilish birds within the kingdom tree, the kingdom lump of dough has sinful leaven mixed into it.

3. **The apostle Paul uses the same symbol to mean sin.** Twice he speaks of leaven working through a lump of dough (1 Corinthians 5:6; Galatians 5:9) and both times leaven represents infecting sin. This is the same way Jesus speaks of leaven.

Leaven consistently symbolizes sin in the Bible and so leaven had to be expelled during the Feast of Passover to picture the perfect purity of Christ.

Bitter Herbs

The Israelites ate bitter herbs in their Passover meal as a symbol of their bitter slavery. Modern Jews eat horseradish or something like it that is spicy enough to bring a tear to the eye. This recalls the many years of weeping as the Hebrew people endured their forced labor.

The bitter herbs also anticipated the coming Messiah who would suffer a cruel death on a cross. He would be "a man of sorrows, and acquainted with grief" (Isaiah 53:3).

The Lord's Passover

This was the Lord's Passover. The Lord passed over the houses with the blood on the doors. There was no distinction made between Jew and Egyptian. It is possible that some Egyptians took warning from the nine previous plagues and joined with the Hebrews in putting blood on their doors. Ancestry did not matter, whether one was part of the oppressed people or a member of the ruling class. The only thing that decided between life and death in a household was the blood.

The blood is the criteria for us still today. It does not matter what family we are born into, what church we may attend, what works we may have performed, when or how we were baptized, or whether we are good people. When judgment time comes the only thing that saves is the blood of Christ.

A Day to Commemorate

God remembered his people and his covenant with Abraham. The Jews remember how God delivered them from cruel Egyptian bondage, establishing Passover as a memorial. Each annual slaughter of the lambs is not meant to secure once again Israel's freedom. Passover is an annual reminder of that freedom that was won for them one time many years ago.

And so it is with Christ's death on the cross. He died once for all to save us from our sins. The book of Hebrews makes much of this point, that Jesus died only once, that Christ *cannot* be crucified again (Hebrews 6:6; 10:1-18).

The Timing of Passover

As we can see there are many details of the Passover celebration that pointed directly to Christ. But there are many other aspects of the Passover than the ones we have listed. There are even traditions that have grown up in the Passover Seder outside of the Bible that also seem to picture Jesus. But one of the more prominent features of God's commands for the Passover is the timing of these events.

On the 10th day of the first month the Israelites were to set apart a perfect lamb without spot or blemish. Then all Israel slaughtered the lambs on the evening of the 14th. This was the night of their deliverance. God is very specific about these dates for a reason. And that reason would have to be that it foretells what Jesus will do. But this is where there has been a great amount of debate over the centuries as to the specific day Jesus was crucified. Tradition says that Jesus died on what we call Good Friday and rose on Sunday, the first day of the week. The problem with this view is that it plays fast and loose with Jesus' prediction that, like Jonah inside the fish, he would be *three days and three nights* in the grave (Matthew 12:40). No matter how one counts, it is impossible to find three nights between Friday and Sunday. So either Jesus spoke figuratively, he was misquoted, or he did not die on Friday.

The feasts give us the answer as to what happened during Jesus' Passion Week. On the 10th of the month the Jews set apart their lambs. This was an act of faith before that first Passover when the Jews were slaves in Egypt. It identified a person as part of the "Israelite freedom group." Passersby would hear the young lamb bleating and see it tied alone or penned up away from the flock. They would know that the person in that house was a follower of Moses, someone in favor of the release of the Jews. This was a step of faith taken prior to seeing God's deliverance. But that is what a step of faith is, an act of obedience to God that depends on what God said he would do. The Israelites had seen nine miraculous plagues afflict the Egyptians, but they didn't have to do anything with any of those. They simply watched as God displayed his awesome power. Now they had to take action to determine which side of the plague they would be on. But this again is exactly how faith is. God does not ask us to make a total blind leap into the unknown. He shows us good reason for trusting him, then he asks us to step out in faith, believing that he will do what he says.

Just as the Hebrew slaves set apart their lambs for that first Passover, the Jews set apart the ultimate Passover Lamb on the 10th day of the first month in another year. On the first day of the week prior to his crucifixion, the day we now commemorate as Palm Sunday, Jesus rode a donkey into Jerusalem to shouts of "Hosanna! Blessed is he who comes in the name of the Lord" (John 12:13). On this day when the Jews were choosing their Passover lambs, they also set aside THE Passover Lamb, Jesus.

Since the tenth day of the first month, Nisan 10, fell on the first day of the week that year, we know that the 14th would be on the fifth day of the week, Thursday. John's Gospel makes clear to us that Jesus died on the evening of the 14th, at about 3:00 in the afternoon, the time of the evening sacrifice when the Passover lambs were being slain. If Jesus died on Thursday, then his prophecy of three days and three nights is completely accurate: Thursday, Friday, and Saturday nights make three nights and the three days would be Friday, Saturday, and Sunday. The Passover feast perfectly prophesied what would happen that final week. And I believe a careful reading of the Gospels will show that they are all in agreement with this scenario.

John lays out the events most clearly for us.

When Jesus had received the sour wine, he said, "It is finished," and he bowed his head and gave up his spirit. Since it was the day of Preparation, and so that the bodies would not remain on the cross on the Sabbath (for that Sabbath was a high day), the Jews asked Pilate that their legs might be broken and that they might be taken away.
John 19:30-31

Jesus died, John says, on the day of Preparation. That is the day prior to the Feast of Unleavened Bread. The Jews busily made preparation on this day by removing all leaven from their homes. The next day was a Sabbath, a high day according to John. The first and last days of Unleavened Bread were special Sabbath days. So the day following Jesus' death was a high Sabbath day, the first day of the Feast of Unleavened Bread. This explains why the women could not come to anoint Jesus' body until Sunday morning. Jesus died on Thursday and was hastily laid in the tomb that evening. Friday was a special Sabbath day on which the women could not do the work of anointing his body. The next day was Saturday, the regular weekly Sabbath, and so another day in which they could not go to the tomb. The first opportunity the women got to anoint Jesus' body was on Sunday morning, the first day of the week.

So here is the order of events during the Passion Week as the Gospel of John describes it:

Sunday, Nisan 10	Passover lambs set apart	Jesus' Triumphal Entry
Wednesday, Nisan 13		Last Supper
Thursday, Nisan 14	Passover lambs sacrificed	Jesus' Crucifixion
Friday, Nisan 15	First Day of Unleavened Bread	Special Sabbath
Saturday, Nisan 16	Regular Weekly Sabbath	
Sunday, Nisan 17	First Day of the Week	Jesus' Resurrection

Now we need to look at the other gospels to see if they agree with this arrangement. Mark 15:42 and Luke 23:54 say Jesus died and Joseph of Arimathea placed his body in the tomb on Preparation Day. Matthew 27:62 identifies the next day after Jesus' death to be the day after the Preparation Day. All the Gospel writers agree, therefore, that Jesus died on Preparation Day, the day before the first day of Unleavened Bread.

Of course, there is the problem of the Last Supper. How could Jesus have celebrated the Passover meal with his disciples the previous evening and then been crucified at the time of the Passover sacrifice? While this is difficult, it is not impossible to fit together with this interpretation. But the traditional interpretation of events actually makes no sense at all. This scenario would have Jesus eating the Passover with his disciples on Thursday evening and then being crucified on Friday. The Jews would have had to terribly violate the special Sabbath by having Jesus crucified on that day. That Friday would have been the first day of Unleavened Bread, a special Sabbath. Jesus' enemies had specifically stated that they didn't want to kill him *during* the feast because they were afraid of a riot breaking out among the people (Matthew 26:5, Mark 14:2). So it is highly unlikely that Jesus was crucified on that Friday. Instead, John tells us plainly that Jesus was crucified on the day of the Passover.

> *Then they led Jesus from the house of Caiaphas to the governor's headquarters. It was early morning. They themselves did not enter the governor's headquarters, so that they would not be defiled, but could eat the Passover.*
> **John 18:28**

Jesus' trial before Pilate was early in the morning and he died on the cross that afternoon. Since the leaders that brought him to Pilate were concerned about keeping themselves ceremonially clean and able to eat the feast, we know the Passover had not yet occurred.

So how could Jesus have eaten the Passover the night before his crucifixion? Some interpreters have theorized that it was not a Passover meal. But Matthew, Mark, and Luke all make clear that it really was a Passover meal that Jesus shared with the disciples. Do the Scriptures hopelessly contradict themselves?

Many theories have been offered to deal with the discrepancy over the timing of the Passover when Jesus ate the Last Supper with his disciples. Two explanations seem most plausible.

Paul Billerbeck argues that in the year of Christ's crucifixion there was a dispute between the Pharisees and Sadducees as to when the new moon arrived. Therefore, the Pharisees held that the first month began one day sooner than the Sadducees. This resulted in the Pharisees observing Passover the day before the Sadducees.[3] The only problem with this interpretation is that Billerbeck lacks any evidence that this indeed happened the year Jesus died. And he has no explanation for how the Pharisees would have been able to get their Passover lambs sacrificed a day early at the temple, since it was controlled by the Sadducees.

---

[3] Hermann Leberecht Strack and Paul Billerbeck, *Kommentar zum Neuen Testament aus Talmud und Midrasch,* München: Beck, 1922-1961, vol. II 847-53.

Another possible scenario is proposed by J. Pickl. He states that Galileans regularly sacrificed their Passover lambs a day early, on the 13th, while the people of Judea kept the 14th.[4] This was presumably allowed in order to accommodate the huge number of animals that had to pass through the temple for this feast. Again, the problem is that Pickl lacks specific evidence to support this claim.

But these two explanations are both bolstered by an obscure debate between Jewish rabbis in the first century. The rabbis argued whether a Passover sacrifice called by a different name and offered on a different day would be accepted by God. It seems that some people had brought Passover lambs to sacrifice early and told the attending priest that they were fellowship offerings. The rabbinic council ruled that sacrifices offered under the wrong name or on the wrong day would not be acceptable "except for the Passover and the sin offering."[5] The fact that this issue came up for debate shows that Passover sacrifices were made on a date other than the 14th of Nisan and that such sacrifices were allowed.

---

[4] Joachim Jeremias, *The Eucharistic words of Jesus*, trans. N. Perrin from the German 3rd ed., *Die Abendmahlswort e Jesu* with the author's revision to July 1964, London: SCM, 1966, p. 24.

[5] Maurice Casey, *Aramaic sources of Mark's Gospel*, Society for New Testament studies monograph series 102, Cambridge: CUP, 1998, pp. 223-25. These conclusions were first published as "The Date Of The Passover Sacrifices And Mark 14:12" Tyndale Bulletin 48, 1998, pp. 245-47.

So it seems that Jesus could have eaten the Passover one evening and then been crucified at the time of the Passover sacrifice the next day. But there are still some other verses that raise questions. In Matthew 26:17 we read that on the first day of the Feast of Unleavened Bread Jesus sent his disciples to prepare the Passover. Strictly speaking, this cannot fit with everything else we have been told. The first day of the Feast of Unleavened Bread is the day *following* Passover. So Matthew tells us that Jesus was crucified on the day prior to the feast and that he ate the Last Supper on the first day of the feast. This would mean that he was crucified the day before he ate the supper.

To understand this we need to recognize how the Jews spoke of the feasts. While Passover and Unleavened Bread were two feasts, they were so closely linked to one another that often the one term, the Feast of Unleavened Bread, was used to refer to both the Passover meal and the seven days of Unleavened Bread that followed. Mark 14:12 also says that on the first day of Unleavened Bread Jesus sent his disciples to prepare the Passover meal, but it further specifies that this was the day that it was customary to sacrifice the lamb. So obviously Mark is not speaking strictly of the seven days of Unleavened Bread, he has included the day of the Passover sacrifice as the first day of the Feast of Unleavened Bread.

Still the skeptic could point out that this scenario also has Jesus eating the Passover meal on the same day as he is crucified at the time of the Passover sacrifice. Again the preceding hypothesis would supply an answer. Since the Jews often included the day of the Passover as part of the Feast of Unleavened Bread, and if there was a custom or an allowance for certain people to celebrate the Passover a day early, then it would be logical to consider that day as the first day of Unleavened Bread.

Therefore, Jesus could have eaten the Passover meal on the 13th of the month. Possibly this happened because the Pharisees reckoned the beginning of the month a day early as Billerbeck suggests. Or it might have been because Galileans, according to Pickl, were allowed to have the supper a day early to ease overcrowding. Either way, it is perfectly reasonable to think that Jesus could have celebrated the Passover with his disciples on the 13th and then been crucified at the time of the Passover sacrifice on the 14th.

That Jesus ate the Passover the night before, on the 13th of the month, is possibly hinted at in Matthew's account.

He said, "Go into the city to a certain man and say to him, 'The Teacher says, My time is at hand. I will keep the Passover at your house with my disciples.'"
Matthew 26:18

We normally assume that when Jesus says, "My time is at hand," he is talking about his time for crucifixion. That may be what he means here, but it is not necessarily so. Why would it matter to the owner of the house that Jesus' time to die was near? How would he know anything about that? But it would make sense if he were renting out his home for travelers to celebrate Passover. Jesus' time is at hand, according to the Pharisaic reckoning of the day of the month or according to the Galilean tradition he is following. The disciples tell the man that their appointed time, the time set for them to have the Passover meal, is near so they need to have access to the room to make preparations.

If Jesus means that his appointed time to observe the meal is at hand, all the apparent discrepancies in the text disappear. Many see disparities in the Scriptures and immediately assume the writers were uninformed, mistaken, or deliberately deceptive. A better approach is to take the biblical text as it is and give it the benefit of the doubt where we lack complete information. Although we cannot absolutely verify that this is what happened, it is quite plausible that Jesus ate the Passover with his disciples on the 13th and then was crucified at the time of the slaughter of the lambs on the 14th.

Establishing the time of Jesus' crucifixion is important because it emphasizes how Jesus fulfilled the first four feasts on the particular days they were celebrated. The New Testament clearly tells us that Pentecost and Firstfruits were fulfilled on the particular dates of the feast days, and John carefully tells us that Passover was fulfilled on the day and at the very hour the lambs were slain. God very pointedly chose the specific days for the feasts to picture perfectly what Christ would accomplish and when he would do it.

The Passover Offering

In the last chapter we mentioned that each feast featured a different type of offering. Obviously the Passover lamb takes center stage here. But what kind of offering was the Passover? What did God reveal by this particular sacrifice?

The dominant characteristic of the sin offering was the sprinkled blood while the special feature of the fellowship offering was the shared meal. Obviously both of these things are important in the Passover sacrifice, so some have concluded that the Passover was a type of hybrid offering containing elements of both sin offering and fellowship offering.

But there is something else going on here. In the sin offering, after the blood was drained and sprinkled and a portion of the animal was burned on the altar fire, the rest of the animal became the property of the priests. The priests, and only the priests, would then dine on the flesh of the sin offering. When God commands every Israelite to eat of the Passover lamb, the sin offering, he is establishing the whole community of Israel as priests. And that is what they are, a kingdom of priests. God very pointedly tells Moses exactly this.

> *and you shall be to me a kingdom of priests and a holy nation. These are the words that you shall speak to the people of Israel.*
> **Exodus 19:6**

Passover was the defining event that constituted Israel as a nation and it constituted them as a nation of priests. The Passover lamb was a sin offering whose blood was sprinkled to deliver from sin and whose flesh was eaten by the priests, the whole nation of Israel.

That the Passover lamb was a sin offering has further significance when Jesus institutes a new observance out of the meal. At the last supper he took the bread and the cup and commanded his followers to do this in remembrance of him. All Jesus' followers are to partake of this memorial supper that recalls Christ's sacrifice on the cross, just like all

Israelites eat the Passover lamb that remembers the night of their deliverance from slavery. Thus Peter says the church is now "a royal priesthood" (1 Peter 2:9). We no longer need a priest to mediate between a holy God and our sinful selves. Jesus is our great High Priest that makes us confident to enter into the Lord's presence (Hebrews 4:16). All who trust in Christ's atoning blood are transformed into believer-priests who can approach God directly.

Passover was a once for all sin offering that delivered Israel from death, won them freedom from slavery, and constituted them as God's nation of priests. Now in the Lord's Supper we celebrate the once for all sin offering of Christ on the cross that delivered us from death, won us freedom from slavery to sin, and constituted us as God's royal priesthood. Jesus, the Passover Lamb, the sin offering, justified us before a holy God. Because the Judge looks at the blood sprinkled on our behalf, we are declared not guilty.

Chapter 3: The Feast of Unleavened Bread

> *And on the fifteenth day of the same month is the Feast of Unleavened bread to the LORD; for seven days you shall eat unleavened bread. On the first day you shall have a holy convocation; you shall not do any ordinary work. But you shall present a food offering to the LORD for seven days. On the seventh day is a holy convocation; you shall not do any ordinary work.*
> **Leviticus 23:6-8**

In the last chapter we began studying the feasts of Israel with Passover. Passover pictures our salvation from slavery to sin. Most people have heard of Passover, but they may not know anything about the feast that comes right on its heels, Unleavened Bread.

The Feast of Unleavened Bread is the first example of the "backward theologizing" we hope to correct with this book. Some commentators have recognized that Passover was ultimately fulfilled by Jesus' death on the cross and the Feast of Firstfruits by his resurrection. Since Jesus' burial in the tomb is what happened between his crucifixion and resurrection, they conclude that the Feast of Unleavened Bread, coming between Passover and Firstfruits, was fulfilled by his burial.

How can the Feast of Unleavened Bread picture the dead body of Christ being placed in a tomb? If the festival had been held for three days we would see a correlation to the three days in the grave. But it is not celebrated for three days, it is seven. What is there in the Feast of Unleavened Bread that connects to Jesus' burial? There is nothing. We must not simply force the feasts onto the events that took place many years later. We must begin with the feasts and move to the future.

Here in Leviticus 23:6 we read that the Feast of Unleavened Bread began the next day, immediately after the Passover. It was a seven day festival with the first and last days being set aside as Sabbaths. The book of Numbers (Numbers 28:19-22) specifies that on each day of Unleavened Bread there was a burnt offering of two bulls, one ram, and seven lambs plus a sin offering of one goat. This is exactly the same requirement as for the first day of each month. It emphasizes sanctification, with the bulk of the animals being completely consumed on the altar fire in a burnt offering. This was appropriate for the new moon sacrifice that marked the first day of the month, consecrating the entire month to God. But it is also appropriate for the Feast of Unleavened Bread because this feast pictures the sanctifying, or setting apart, of God's people to himself. As we concluded in chapter 1, this offering envisions the consecration of all God's people, both Jew and Gentile. And that is what Unleavened Bread pictures, the setting apart of Israel in service to God as well as the ultimate calling of all kinds of people from all nations into God's family.

But the sacrifices offered on the altar are really only supplementary and secondary to the eating of unleavened bread. The banishment of leaven or yeast is central in this celebration. Historically, the feast recalls Israel's hasty exodus from Egypt when they had no time to allow their bread to rise. But theologically, it represents God's sanctification of a special people. Throughout the Bible, leaven is used as a metaphor for sin (Matthew 16:12;

1 Corinthians 5:8). Yeast starts small but eventually works its way completely through a lump of dough, affecting the whole. Removing the sinful leaven represents God's removal of sin from his people. And as God separates his people from worldly Egypt, he commands the separation of the bread from the infecting leaven.

The 7 Days of Unleavened Bread

Why is the Feast of Unleavened Bread seven days? Most holidays occupy only one day. They may be anniversaries of a significant event and are celebrated on the date of its occurrence. For example, America's Independence Day is July 4 because it is the anniversary of the adoption of the Declaration of Independence. In the same way, Passover is Nisan 14 because that is the day Israel was delivered from Egypt. So it makes sense for a holiday to be set aside on the anniversary of an historic event.

The date of a holiday's observance can also be established as just an agreed upon day to remember important things. In the United States, Memorial Day and Thanksgiving do not fall on anniversary dates. They are special days set aside to remember those who gave their lives for our country and to give thanks for our blessings, respectively.

But a seven day holiday is very unusual. We might think of another week long celebration, Hanukkah, the Festival of Lights that lasts eight days. But Hanukkah is also an anniversary celebration recalling the eight day miracle when the little bit of oil burned for over a week, symbolizing God's approval of the Maccabean Jews' efforts to cleanse the temple. The eight days of Hanukkah are very significant to its celebration. Thus there is an historical reason for the holiday lasting over a week.

Is there an historical reason for the Feast of Unleavened Bread to last seven days? The feast commemorated Israel's abrupt exit from Egypt when there was no time to allow the bread to rise. The Israelites were on the run with pharaoh on their tail until the miraculous crossing of the Red Sea. Once the Egyptian army was drowned, Israel finally had some breathing room and could possibly have had the luxury then to let the bread rise. Do the seven days of Unleavened Bread correspond with the time between the exodus and the crossing of the sea? Do they remember the exact period of time that the Jews' flight from Egypt prohibited their being able to let the bread rise? This is possible, but the Bible does not tell us exactly how long it took to travel to the edge of the sea or what day it was that they crossed over. Exodus does not specify a reason from historical events for Unleavened Bread being seven days.

Since the Exodus narrative gives no historical reason for the Feast of Unleavened Bread to be seven days, we must look elsewhere. We are left only with the number seven as a clue to the reason. And that number immediately suggests creation.

Unleavened Bread is a New Creation

God created the world in seven days. This is a foundational truth presented in the Scriptures. Anytime we read of a seven day period it should remind us of creation. Considering creation, it makes perfect sense why the Feast of Unleavened Bread should be seven days long. By delivering the Hebrews from Egypt, God created a new people. He took a loosely connected, large family and constituted a new nation. He freed a bunch of slaves and made a new kingdom. Unleavened Bread lasts seven days because it represents the creation of Israel as a unique nation belonging to God.

When Jesus came as the ultimate Passover Lamb, he accomplished the work that the Feast of Passover had been anticipating for centuries. He also subsequently fulfilled what the Feast of Unleavened Bread predicted, the setting apart of a new people. Because of Jesus' sacrificial death on the cross, anyone in Christ is a new creation (2 Corinthians 5:17). By taking the punishment for our sin, Jesus has created a new people. He has freed us from our bondage to enter into his kingdom. He has welcomed us into his family.

Not only does God create a new people, he also begins creating a new world. God's new creation, those who are in Christ, are given the ministry of reconciliation (2 Corinthians 5:18). That is, we become agents of the new creation, spreading the word about how all people can be made new in Christ and extending God's kingdom in this world.

After God had finished all the work of creation, he rested on the seventh day (Genesis 2:2). On that seventh day of creation everything in the world worked like it was supposed to. Adam and Eve may have sinned on the eighth day, or maybe they lived in perfect harmony and bliss longer than that before they were tempted and fell. We don't know. All we can absolutely be certain of is that the seventh day was an absolutely perfect day in which everything God had created operated according to his will. Because God's work was finished, everything perfectly played out according to the work God had completed.

Just before Jesus died on the cross, he said "It is finished" (John 19:30). He finished his work of redemption that transforms those who believe in him into a new creation. And just as the completion of his work of creation led to everything operating as it should, the end of Jesus' work of redemption should lead to his new creation operating just as it should. Because of Christ's death on the cross, we are empowered to live holy lives. We are his disciples following after his example. We are his body walking in his righteousness. We are his ambassadors sharing his message with the world.

The first and last days of the Feast of Unleavened Bread were designated as Sabbaths. This framed the whole week and in a sense set apart the entire seven days as a Sabbath. When God was finished with the work of creation he rested. Likewise when Jesus completed the work of redemption he declared it was finished and rested. The seven days of Unleavened Bread represent this rest provided by Christ's death on the cross. The writer of the book of Hebrews urges his readers to be sure to enter that rest and not miss it as the unbelieving generation of Israelites did when they refused to enter Canaan.

So then, there remains a Sabbath rest for the people of God, for whoever has entered God's rest has also rested from his works as God did from his.
Hebrews 4:9-10

Trusting in Jesus means resting from your works. Instead of vainly working to prove oneself worthy before a holy God, we rest from those labors in the completed work of our Savior. The Feast of Unleavened Bread follows Passover as a picture of our salvation. When we trust in the sacrifice of Jesus our sins are forgiven, nailed to the cross. We are made new creations and, just as Passover led directly into Unleavened Bread, immediately we enter into Christ's rest (Matthew 11:28).

On the original Sabbath, God's creation worked exactly as it was made to. Now, as a result of Christ's work on the cross, his people have been remade and can work as they were meant to. We are made into the righteousness of Christ and no longer are enslaved to sin, completely incapable of any righteous act (Isaiah 64:6). As unbelievers we had no alternative but simply followed the sin inherent in our nature. But as believers we can choose the right and reject the wrong. Just as Adam and Eve had the choice between good and evil in the perfect Sabbath rest of Eden, now Christians have that same option laid before them in the rest our Lord provides. We are called continually to choose the Spirit and turn from the flesh as we grow into the likeness of Christ.

The feasts of Passover and Unleavened Bread are inseparably linked together, so much so that some commentators conclude that they were really just one festival. This view is bolstered by the fact that the leaven had to be removed before the Passover and then was forbidden for the entire week of Unleavened Bread. Common usage among the Jews could refer to the entire week by the name of either feast. Thus, the term Passover could include the meal and the seven days of Unleavened Bread. And the entire week-long celebration, including the Passover meal, could be meant when simply saying Unleavened Bread.

The two feasts are also linked because of their historical referent. The Jews were delivered from Egyptian slavery on the night of the Passover and subsequently fled in great haste into the desert with no time for their bread to rise, thus giving the occasion for Unleavened Bread.

Spiritually these two feasts picture our salvation. Passover is the salvation event, the defining moment when Israel was freed from slavery. It illustrates that moment in the life of the sinner when grace is applied and the person passes from death into life. Then Unleavened Bread is the Christian life. Like the Jews, we walk out of slavery into freedom. We feed on the unleavened bread that represents the righteousness of Christ (John 6:32-35). And this life stretches out into eternity as indicated by the eight total days of the two feasts. Passover was on the 14th of the month and Unleavened Bread lasted from the 15th through the 21st. That makes eight days. Seven days represented completion as God created the world in that time. The eighth day, therefore, represented a new beginning and that which reaches beyond the whole, eternity.

Unleavened Bread is a New Consecration

But creation is not the only significant seven day period in the Bible. A consecration period also lasted seven days. Consecration involved purification and separation. It was about setting something or someone apart for a special purpose.

Numbers 19 contains the instructions for preparing the water of purification and the regulations for using it. Anyone in the Old Testament community who became defiled through contact with unclean things was quarantined outside the camp for a week and had to be sprinkled with the water of cleansing on the third and seventh days. Only after undergoing this consecration period could the person return to full participation in the worship and life of the community.

This consecration ritual was not a rare occurrence. A common defilement was contact with a dead body. Anyone touching a dead body, and even anyone in a house where someone died, had to go through this process. So it was almost guaranteed that everyone in Israel at some time or another would need to be cleansed in this way.

This universal need for cleansing pictures the state of all humanity. All have sinned, we are all under the curse of death. Therefore we all need consecration or purification from the stench of death. Jesus said that anyone that he does not wash cannot have a part in him (John 13:8). So the seven days of the Feast of Unleavened Bread represent the consecration period in which Christ cleans up his people, uniting them with himself and welcoming them into full fellowship.

But the symbolism goes even further. Consecration meant not only purification, but also separation to special service. Leviticus 8 describes the ordination of Aaron and his sons to serve as priests. After the sacrifices had been offered and the blood had been sprinkled, Aaron and his sons had to remain in the presence of God at the tent of meeting for seven days. This week-long ordination set them apart as priests to God.

Likewise, the Feast of Unleavened Bread is seven days because all Israel was consecrated to God as a kingdom of priests. After the Passover lambs were sacrificed for each family and the blood was sprinkled on each doorway, the Israelites spent a week eating only unleavened bread in the presence of God, who appeared in the pillar of cloud and the pillar of fire. The feast was a seven day ordination period just like Aaron and his sons went through.

Israel's ordination as a kingdom of priests was prelude to the ultimate consecration God had planned. When Jesus died on the cross as **the** Passover Lamb and his blood was sprinkled for our pardon, he consecrated a new kingdom of priests. The Feast of Unleavened Bread lasts seven days because it pictures the ordination of all believers in Christ into the gospel ministry.

The Lesson of the Feast of Unleavened Bread

There is some debate over the timing of Passover and Unleavened Bread. Some hold that the Passover meal was to be eaten on what we would consider the evening of the 13th of Nisan. In the Hebrew mind, a day began with evening and was followed by morning (Genesis 1:5). Therefore, the day begins about 6:00 p.m. instead of at midnight. So the evening of the 14th would mean as the sun was going down on the 13th and the calendar was changing to the 14th. In this interpretation, the Israelites would have slaughtered their lambs and placed the blood on the doors as the day was changing from the 13th to the 14th. During the night pharaoh released them and they left Egypt, traveling into the desert on the 14th of Nisan. After walking for a day, they would have stopped to observe a Sabbath on the 15th of Nisan, the first day of the Feast of Unleavened Bread. Then they would have continued their journey on the 16th of the month. The following chart illustrates this view.

Evening of Nisan 14	Morning of Nisan 14	Nisan 15	Nisan 16
Slaughter lambs and eat Passover	Walk out of Egypt	Observe Sabbath for the first day of Unleavened Bread	Continue journey into desert

Proponents of this theory point out that if the Passover was eaten at the end of Nisan 14, then the Israelites would have begun their journey out of Egypt on the first day of the Feast of Unleavened Bread, a day that God commanded to be a Sabbath. Keeping the Sabbath included not walking farther than what became known as "a Sabbath day's walk" (Acts 1:12), which was roughly about ¾ of a mile. So it is assumed that the Israelites could not have walked into the desert on that Sabbath day, for they would only have been able to travel about ¾ of a mile.

But this reasoning is anachronistic. Anachronism means taking something from a later time and applying it to a previous time, like putting tennis shoes on Abraham. The idea that the children of Israel could not travel more than a short distance on a Sabbath places restrictions on the Hebrews leaving Egypt that were not established until sometime later. Jewish teachers derived the idea of the Sabbath day's walk from passages like Numbers 35:4-5 and Joshua 3:4. Neither of these Scriptures had been written at the time of the exodus. Furthermore, the Sabbath day's walk is Jewish tradition developed from interpretations of Scripture, it is not a clear command found in the Bible. So it is incorrect to assume that the Hebrew slaves were restricted by the injunction against travel on the Sabbath.

While it is true that evening precedes morning in Hebrew thinking, it is not true that the Passover sacrifice on the evening of Nisan 14 means the beginning of that day. Numbers 28:4 speaks of the daily sacrifices and places the morning sacrifice *before* the evening sacrifice. Clearly an evening sacrifice on Nisan 14 would take place at the end of the day as the calendar moved to the 15th.

But Moses removes all doubt about when the Israelites left Egypt. He summarizes all their travels in Numbers 33. At the beginning of that chapter he plainly states that the Israelites marched out of Egypt on the 15th day of the first month, the day after the Passover (Numbers 33:3).

Actually the Hebrews' flight on a Sabbath was all part of the picture God was painting with the feasts. The Israelites did travel on that first day of the Feast of Unleavened Bread because it beautifully illustrates the reality God is communicating. As we have seen, Passover pictures our salvation through the redemption Jesus purchased for us on the cross, our justification. Immediately following Passover is Unleavened Bread that pictures sanctification. After Israel was delivered from slavery they walked out into freedom led by God's guidance with the pillar of cloud and of fire. They obediently followed the Lord after being delivered from slavery. Likewise, after accepting the salvation Jesus provides, the new Christian is to walk in newness of life following the Savior. The Israelites' journey perfectly pictures our new life in Christ. Therefore, the events commemorated by Passover and Unleavened Bread happened as this chart describes.

End of Nisan 14	Nisan 15	Nisan 16 and following
Slaughter lambs and eat Passover	Walk out of Egypt	Continue journey into desert

In our evangelical tradition we have been very good on Passover, the salvation event. We have majored on evangelism and the need for a personal salvation experience. We have ordered our worship services so that they climax with a call to respond to the gospel.

But we often fail to emphasize the life of growing to be like Christ that should come from that event. We have treated salvation as fire insurance. Once we have it we don't think about it until disaster strikes. We have allowed regeneration to be like a wedding without a marriage. The wedding may be a wonderful, glamorous event, but then what if the couple forgets that it is supposed to lead into a lifetime of marriage? How ridiculous for a bride and groom to share vows with one another and then return to their separate lives.

The salvation experience (the wedding) that is not followed by the believer's daily commitment to Christ (the marriage) can happen because the incredible high of salvation is then followed by a spiritual life that doesn't have the same thrill. There may be difficult times as the new Christian's old environment and ways clash with her new standing in Christ. Just as the Jews' incredible deliverance from slavery led to walking in the desert, our exciting conversion experience leads to a daily walk with Christ that may be less than desirable. Often we face the painful process of allowing God to transform us, cutting out our bad behaviors and attitudes. We are suddenly compelled to choose obedience to Christ by doing what we wouldn't normally choose. We are called to follow him wherever he leads, even if it's out into the hot and dry desert.

Unleavened Bread is the boring cousin of Passover. But it is absolutely necessary. The two feasts demonstrate the relationship between grace and works. Our salvation is completely the work of God (Passover) but it leads to a life of following Christ (Unleavened Bread).

The book of Hebrews warns that we not be like the Jews who experienced the wonderful deliverance of Passover but then proved themselves faithless by refusing to enter the Promised Land (Hebrews 4:1). If Passover is not followed by Unleavened Bread, there is no salvation.

Jesus calls to the wayward children of Israel saying,

> *"Come to me, all who labor and are heavy laden, and I will give you rest. Take my yoke upon you, and learn from me, for I am gentle and lowly in heart, and you will find rest for your souls. For my yoke is easy, and my burden is light."*
>
> **Matthew 11:28-30**

Followers of Jesus are like weary, abused oxen whom the Good Master, Jesus, purchases and invites into his service. He promises rest or Sabbath for anyone who comes to him. Yet this rest does not mean inactivity. Christ has work for his people to do. But unlike their cruel former master, Jesus' yoke is easy and his burden is light. Entry into Christ's rest is followed by serving in his field. Passover is followed by Unleavened Bread.

The apostle Paul writes,

> *For by grace you have been saved through faith. And this is not your own doing; it is the gift of God, not a result of works, so that no one may boast. For we are his workmanship, created in Christ Jesus for good works, which God prepared beforehand, that we should walk in them.*
>
> **Ephesians 2:8-10**

God saves us so that we might do the works he planned for us to do. Unleavened Bread pictures our walk in the good works prepared for us.

James tells us that if confession of faith is not followed by a changed life, there is no salvation.

For as the body apart from the spirit is dead, so also faith apart from works is dead.

James 2:26

If faith does not express itself with works of righteousness, it is worthless. This is the message of Unleavened Bread.

Thus the Feast of Unleavened Bread pictures the life of faith growing out of the salvation event. The Israelites ate the first Passover and were delivered from Egyptian slavery that very night. The next day they followed Moses out into the desert, walking out of slavery and into freedom. But that freedom was not a cake walk. They had to travel through the desert, facing hardships and learning to trust the benevolent hand of their mighty God to provide the most basic necessities.

In the same way, when we place our faith in the sacrificial death of Christ it is like we are placing the blood of the Lamb on our doors. Then we must follow after Christ, day by day, as he leads us through the difficult desert of life in this fallen world to our Sabbath rest.

Chapter 4: The Feast of Firstfruits

> *And the LORD spoke to Moses, saying, "Speak to the people of Israel and say to them, When you come into the land that I give you and reap its harvest, you shall bring the sheaf of the firstfruits of your harvest to the priest, and he shall wave the sheaf before the LORD, so that you may be accepted. On the day after the Sabbath the priest shall wave it. And on the day when you wave the sheaf, you shall offer a male lamb a year old without blemish as a burnt offering to the LORD. And the grain offering with it shall be two tenths of an ephah of fine flour mixed with oil, a food offering to the LORD with a pleasing aroma, and the drink offering with it shall be of wine, a fourth of a hin. And you shall eat neither bread nor grain parched or fresh until this same day, until you have brought the offering of your God: it is a statute forever throughout your generations in all your dwellings.*
> **Leviticus 23:9-14**

Growing up in church I don't ever recall hearing anything about the Feast of Firstfruits. Passover certainly got some attention when we talked about Moses, and Pentecost was celebrated, although I'm not sure I really understood that Pentecost was a Jewish festival long before it became the birthday of the church. I also heard about the Day of Atonement and a little about the Feast of Tabernacles. But I don't think I ever heard any mention of Firstfruits or what event it prophesied.

The Firstfruits Honors God

Leviticus 23:9-14 outlines the Feast of Firstfruits. When the Israelites began harvesting in the spring they were to bring a sheaf of the first ripened grain and wave it before the Lord on the day after the Sabbath. The wave offering was just what it sounds like. The sacrifice being waved was lifted up before God and waved in the air. When offerings were burned on the altar we can easily see the symbolism of the smoke rising, thus the sacrifice is going up to God who enjoys the sweet smell. But what did the wave offering mean?

We can liken the significance of the wave offering to a large family opening presents on Christmas morning. Suppose Sally opens a gift from her Aunt Marie, exactly the sweater she had admired in the store when she went shopping with her aunt. She looks up and sees Aunt Marie all the way on the other side of the room, separated by all the Christmas commotion of brothers, sisters, and cousins ripping open packages. Sally lifts the sweater up in the air and waves it to catch her aunt's attention as she calls out "Thank you!" Aunt Marie sees her delight with her gift and is pleased that Sally has received what she meant her to have.

When God's people brought their sheaves of new grain and waved them before him, they were saying "Thank you!" And God was pleased with their gratitude and recognition that he is the Source of their blessing.

Notice again that this offering is in response to what God has already done. There is no ceremony or ritual performed in order to obtain God's blessing of the harvest. Instead, there is a response of thanksgiving for the crops that God has graciously provided. So the first grain cut from the field was brought to the tabernacle or temple to be waved before the Lord, demonstrating the people's thanksgiving. This was done on the day after the Sabbath, the first day of the week.

Firstfruits is about honoring God. Just as the proper host will serve his honored guest at the table first, the Israelites could not begin to enjoy the bread and other good things from their grain until they had offered the first portion to God. He deserves the first and the best, never the leftovers.

The offering of firstfruits was made on the day after the Sabbath, the first day of the week, Sunday. Not only is it the first of the grain that is offered, it is offered as the first duty of the week. This is possibly what the apostle Paul had in mind when he instructed the Corinthian church to set aside their offering every week on the first day of the week (1 Corinthians 16:2). Giving to God first emphasizes the priority the Lord takes in our lives. We even here have Old Testament justification for Sunday worship. When we gather on the first day of the week to offer our sacrifices of praise, thanksgiving, and tithes we are following this biblical precedent of placing God first in our lives. We worship on the first day to remind us to live each day of the week in obedience to our Lord.

The Firstfruits Anticipates Greater Blessing

With the waving of the first ripening barley the worshiper is also looking forward in faith to the year's full harvest. Firstfruits begins the counting of Sabbaths until Pentecost 50 days later that celebrates the arrival of the wheat when the harvest season is in full swing. So the Israelites not only looked back in gratitude for what God had provided, but also forward to the greater blessing that was still to come.

This feast taught the principle that honoring God with the firstfruits of what we earn or receive leads to greater blessing. The book of Proverbs instructs

> *Honor the LORD with your wealth and with the firstfruits of all your produce; then your barns will be filled with plenty, and your vats will be bursting with wine.*
> **Proverbs 3:9-10**

The basic idea of this proverb is that we are to recognize the Source of our blessings and offer back the first and best of what God has given us. Then he promises to continue pouring out more blessings.

Unfortunately, this principle has been abused by many fund raisers and preachers of a so-called "health and wealth" doctrine. We must remember that **this is a proverb, not a promise**. God does not say there is an absolute one to one correlation between our giving and our receiving, this is more of a general rule. We can easily find exceptions to the rule: faithful, generous believers that were destitute. Think of Job or any of those heroes of the faith listed in Hebrews 11 who went about with nothing, living in holes in the ground. And Jesus himself stated that he had no place to lay his head. So we must not think of the offering of firstfruits as a guaranteed investment that will bring a hefty return. That is never to be our motivation for giving. Just as we have noted before, our offerings to God are always in response to his grace, they are never inducements to procure greater blessing. You can't bribe God.

While the offer of firstfruits is not a guarantee of greater blessing in the physical world, there is a direct correlation in the spiritual realm. Jesus advised that you

> *lay up for yourselves treasures in heaven, where neither moth nor rust destroys and where thieves do not break in and steal.*
> **Matthew 6:20**

Again he says,

> *For to the one who has, more will be given, and he will have an abundance*
> **Matthew 13:12**

Obedience to Christ always pays off. We may not see it in this world because of the stain of sin. But in heaven and in the new world to come, there will always be the multiplication of blessing for the faithful.

The Firstfruits is Christ

Christ's resurrection fulfilled the Feast of Firstfruits. This festival followed the death of winter and celebrated the new life springing forth from the earth. The Lord commanded that the sheaf be waved on the day after the Sabbath. Justin Martyr wrote "The first day after the Sabbath, remaining the first of all the days, is called, however, the eighth, according to the number of all the days of the cycle, and [yet] remains the first."[6] Since the Sabbath was the seventh day, the day after could be understood as the eighth day. Seven days represented the completion of the creation, now the eighth

---

[6] Justin Martyr, *Dialogue with Trypho*, chapter XLI.

day is symbolic of a new beginning, new life in the new year, a new creation.

Just as the sheaf was presented before the Lord on the day after the Sabbath, Jesus rose on the first day of the week. God could have required the Firstfruits as part of Sabbath observance, but he very pointedly instructed that it be brought the first day of the week in anticipation of the resurrection. Christ is the firstfruits from the dead raised on the exact day of the Feast of Firstfruits, just as he gave up the Spirit at the exact time of the sacrifice of the Passover lamb.

According to Leviticus 23:12 a burnt offering of a lamb accompanied the sheaf of grain. This clarifies that the sheaf is tied to Passover. The Passover sacrifice secured Israel's freedom from slavery and led to the possession of their own land. The former slaves now have the opportunity to enjoy the harvest from their own fields, and that harvest is celebrated with Firstfruits.

But the sacrifice of a lamb on Firstfruits also looks forward to Christ. Despite the death of Jesus, the Lamb, new life springs forth. Because of the sacrifice of the Passover Lamb on the cross, the new life represented by the sheaf is possible.

The sheaf that was brought was waved before the Lord. It was not burned on the altar as many other sacrifices were. That would not have pictured the Lord rising triumphantly from the grave. Neither is the grain crushed as it is offered, for Christ's sacrifice had already been made on Calvary. Firstfruits does not prophesy the sacrifice of Christ's life, but his victory over death. Just as the sheaf waved signaled hope and life from the coming harvest, Jesus' resurrection is our hope for being raised with spiritual bodies to live with him eternally, a hope that is secure in him.

What is unbelievable is that we have largely ignored the Feast of Firstfruits! How can the church overlook this feast that pictures the resurrection? The resurrection is the defining event of our faith. Paul tells us in 1 Corinthians 15 that without the resurrection our faith is worthless. The resurrection is what sets Christ apart from all messianic pretenders. Other men had claimed greatness, gathered followers, and taught their theology. Then they died, their disciples were dispersed, and their teaching came to nothing. Jesus' mission followed this same trajectory. He appeared as the Son of God, people flocked around him, and he taught them. After his death on the cross, his disciples were cowering in fear for their lives and this Jesus movement looked destined to follow the same course as all the others.

But then came that Sunday morning. With the resurrection everything changed. Jesus' scared, uneducated, ragtag followers were transformed into an unstoppable army that swept across the Roman Empire and forever changed the course of history. The formerly fearful apostles willingly died for the One they knew was alive. The poor country preacher from the little town of Nazareth in the insignificant region of Galilee whose handful of followers deserted him at his death, has become the most influential man that ever lived. And it's all because he didn't stay dead.

We have easily drawn the lines that connect Passover and the crucifixion, recognizing the New Testament references that point this out like John the Baptist's words,

> *Behold, the Lamb of God, who takes away the sin of the world!*
>
> **John 1:29**

But the New Testament also tells us that

> *Christ has been raised from the dead, the **firstfruits** of those who have fallen asleep*
>
> **1 Corinthians 15:20**

How have we not realized that the Feast of Firstfruits was a picture of the resurrection, the basis of our faith?

The Firstfruits Anticipates More

The term "firstfruits" indicates more to come. If Christ was the first it implies there will be a second, third, fourth, and so on. Just like the waving of the sheaf of grain signaled the coming of a bountiful harvest, Christ's bodily resurrection guarantees the resurrection of all those who trust in him.

That is what is being pictured in an obscure passage in Matthew's account of the crucifixion. Just as Jesus dies on the cross, Matthew adds a peculiar note that does not appear in any of the other gospel writers' descriptions.

> *And Jesus cried out again with a loud voice and yielded up his spirit. And behold, the curtain of the temple was torn in two, from top to bottom. And the earth shook, and the rocks were split. The tombs also were opened. And many bodies of the saints who had fallen asleep were raised,*

and coming out of the tombs after his resurrection they went into the holy city and appeared to many.
Matthew 27:50-53

Matthew reports these phenomena at the death of Jesus: the curtain of the temple tore in two, an earthquake shook the ground, splitting rocks and opening up tombs, and many dead saints were raised to life. But Matthew particularly notes that the saints did not appear to people in Jerusalem until *after* Christ's resurrection. This has been a puzzling passage to comprehend.

The Feast of Firstfruits explains what is happening here. Just as the harvest began before the feast day, these dead saints rise before the resurrection of Christ. It is only after Jesus' resurrection that these believers show themselves to people in Jerusalem to bolster their faith, just as the grain harvested was not used until after the sheaf was waved on Firstfruits. Thus, even though these saints rose from the dead prior to Christ's resurrection, the order of events emphasizes that the life they received is completely dependent upon Jesus' victory over death. Even though Christ is the firstfruits, this does not mean that all those faithful saints of the Old Testament will miss out on the resurrection to life. No, they are part of that early harvest that waited for the offering of the firstfruits, Christ. Once Jesus rises up out of the tomb, all those who had gone on before can also enjoy all the blessings of life that Christ won for all who believe.

The rising of these Old Testament saints at Christ's crucifixion also helps us understand the resurrection. Paul very emphatically teaches that there will be a physical, bodily resurrection of believers (1 Corinthians 15). But this resurrection awaits the end of the age when Jesus returns. Then what resurrection did these Old Testament believers receive at the death of Christ? The resurrection to life in heaven. This question will be dealt with in more depth later in the excursus (page 112).

Therefore, the first three feasts of Israel picture the three great aspects of our salvation that Christ secured for us. They are:

- **Justification**-We are declared innocent before a holy God because of Christ's substitutionary death as our Passover Lamb.

- **Sanctification**-We are made holy by being made into the righteousness of Christ, which is symbolized in the Feast of Unleavened Bread.

- **Glorification**-We are certain of being raised to new life in spiritual bodies because Christ is the Firstfruits from the dead.

Chapter 5: The Feast of Weeks or Pentecost

"You shall count seven full weeks from the day after the Sabbath, from the day that you brought the sheaf of the wave offering. You shall count fifty days to the day after the seventh Sabbath. Then you shall present a grain offering of new grain to the LORD. You shall bring from your dwelling places two loaves of bread to be waved, made of two tenths of an ephah. They shall be of fine flour, and they shall be baked with leaven, as firstfruits to the LORD. And you shall present with the bread seven lambs a year old without blemish, and one bull from the herd and two rams. They shall be a burnt offering to the LORD, with their grain offering and their drink offerings, a food offering with a pleasing aroma to the LORD. And you shall offer one male goat for a sin offering, and two male lambs a year old as a sacrifice of peace offerings. And the priest shall wave them with the bread of the firstfruits as a wave offering before the LORD, with the two lambs. They shall be holy to the LORD for the priest. And you shall make proclamation on the same day. You shall hold a holy convocation. You shall not do any ordinary work. It is a statute forever in all your dwelling places throughout your generations.

"And when you reap the harvest of your land, you shall not reap your field right up to its edge, nor shall you gather the gleanings after your harvest. You shall leave them for the poor and for the sojourner: I am the LORD your God."

Leviticus 23:15-22

The church was born on the Day of Pentecost. Just before Jesus' ascension to heaven he instructed his disciples to remain in Jerusalem until they received power to fulfill their mission. For ten days they met together and prayed. Then, at about 9:00 one morning as they were praying, there was a blowing sound that rushed through the house. Flames of fire appeared above their heads as they began to speak in languages they had never known. The Holy Spirit had come and filled the believers in Jesus. They spilled out into the streets of Jerusalem loudly proclaiming in multiple languages the glorious story of Christ's life, death, and resurrection. People were confused at first but then, after Peter preached to the crowd and explained that what was taking place was prophesied long ago, about 3,000 believed the message. This was the Day of Pentecost, the birthday of the church.

But what we Christians often overlook is that Pentecost was a Jewish festival first. That is why there were people gathered in Jerusalem from all over the world on that special day. Pentecost was one of the three most important feasts of the year in which every Jewish male was to appear before the Lord at Jerusalem. (Passover and Tabernacles were the other two pilgrimage festivals.) So it was no accident that the streets of the city were crowded with people from all over the world speaking a wide variety of languages. Hundreds of years before this event, God not only established Pentecost as a picture of how he would begin redeeming his world, he also set up the feast as the means to accomplish a large spiritual harvest on that day and jumpstart the growth of his kingdom.

Pentecost Celebrates the Harvest

Pentecost is a Greek name drawn from the fact that this feast came 50 days after Firstfruits. In the Old Testament it is called the Feast of Weeks. Seven weeks or seven Sabbaths were counted from Firstfruits making 49 days. The 50th day was then declared a special Sabbath, the Feast of Weeks. Firstfruits was the beginning of the harvest and now Weeks celebrates the full spring harvest.

At the Feast of Pentecost two baked loaves of bread were waved before the Lord. Compare this with Firstfruits where a sheaf of raw, unprepared grain was waved, freshly cut from the field. The sheaf was waved in thankful anticipation of the coming fruitful harvest. Now at Pentecost it is not a sheaf of grain but grain that has been threshed, ground into flour, mixed with yeast, kneaded into dough, and baked into loaves. So while Firstfruits was the harvest anticipated, Pentecost is the harvest received. Firstfruits was like the old ketchup commercial where the boy licks his lips as he anxiously watches and waits for the condiment to slowly drip from the bottle while the singers croon, "An-tici-pa-tion! An-tici-pa-a-tion!" Pentecost is that same boy eagerly biting into his ketchup enhanced hamburger.

Likewise, we have seen that Firstfruits was fulfilled with the resurrection of Christ. But that is just the first of great things to come. It is the guarantee of our hope for our own resurrection. Interestingly, the term "firstfruits" is also applied to Pentecost.

*You shall observe the Feast of Weeks, the **firstfruits** of wheat harvest, and the Feast of Ingathering at the year's end.*

Exodus 34:22

*You shall bring from your dwelling places two loaves of bread to be waved, made of two tenths of an ephah. They shall be of fine flour, and they shall be baked with leaven, as **firstfruits** to the LORD.*

Leviticus 23:17

*And the priest shall wave them with the bread of the **firstfruits** as a wave offering before the LORD, with the two lambs. They shall be holy to the LORD for the priest.*

Leviticus 23:20

Just as the Feast of Firstfruits celebrated the barley harvest, Pentecost is basically the firstfruits of the wheat harvest. Pentecost could even be called *Firstfruits, Part 2*. It is really as if the two feasts are one celebration. The festivities begin when the sheaf is waved the day after the Sabbath and then, 50 days later, the celebration continues with the waving of the loaves.

Firstfruits was fulfilled with the resurrection of Christ. But that is just the first of great things to come. It is the guarantee of our own resurrection. Now Pentecost is the realization of the new life in Christ, the reception of the promised Holy Spirit that ensures our ultimate glorification. The Spirit is the earnest of our inheritance, the down payment on eternity (Ephesians 1:13-14). Jesus said if the seed dies then it produces much more (John 12:24). Firstfruits was the shoot poking up through the soil, Pentecost is the full flowering.

The Offering at Pentecost

Numbers 28:27-30 prescribes for the Feast of Pentecost the standard monthly sacrifice of two bulls, one ram, and seven lambs for a burnt offering and one goat for a sin offering. As we have seen, this combination suggests the consecration of all God's people, Jew and Gentile. So it is especially fitting that this sacrifice would be required on the day that prophesied the pouring out of God's Spirit on all types of people. The believers were empowered to speak in various languages, signaling the availability of the gospel to all, regardless of heritage. These sacrifices pictured the reality of Christ sanctifying all types of people for his service.

But a question arises when we read Leviticus 23:18. This verse specifies a burnt offering on the Feast of Pentecost of seven lambs, one bull and two rams. Numbers requires two bulls and one ram while Leviticus says one bull and two rams. Is there a contradiction in the Scriptures?

First, we must recognize the differences in each passage. Leviticus 23 is outlining the feasts and does not include all the necessary offerings. Meanwhile, Numbers 28-29 meticulously lists each offering for each day. Leviticus very generally speaks of making an offering by fire on several of the feasts (Unleavened Bread in verse 8, Trumpets in verse 25, the Day of Atonement in verse 27, and Tabernacles in verse 36). Numbers gives the details of each of those offerings. This suggests that the Leviticus passage is speaking of a different offering than the Numbers passage.

We must also carefully note that the numbers of bulls and rams is not the only difference. There is a difference in the order in which the animals are listed. Leviticus starts with seven lambs while Numbers follows the normal way of listing the monthly sacrifice with the lambs after the bulls and ram. And Leviticus 23:19 adds a fellowship offering of two lambs. So it is quite likely that these are two separate offerings that are each to be presented on the Feast of Pentecost, not differing views as to what was required.

Leviticus 23:18 states that this offering was presented with the two leavened loaves. Numbers does not even speak of the two loaves waved on Pentecost. The offering in Leviticus, then, is a companion sacrifice to the loaves that is separate from the standard monthly sacrifice that was also commanded on that day.

Then what is being communicated with this Pentecost offering? The Israelites were to present seven lambs, one bull, and two rams as a burnt offering along with one goat for a sin offering and two lambs for a fellowship offering. We have previously seen that the seven lambs represent the Gentile church on other occasions, so we might assume that is the case here as well. That brings us to the one bull and two rams.

The combination of one bull and two rams was first used in the ordination of Aaron and his sons (Exodus 29:1; Leviticus 8:2). With this trio of sacrificial animals the priests were consecrated for service to the Lord. The offering of one bull and two rams suggests, then, that priests are being ordained on this day. And that is exactly what is happening. By pouring out his Spirit on all flesh, God has ordained a new priesthood. All believers regardless of ethnicity, represented by the seven lambs, have been ordained as a nation of priests to serve the Lord (1 Peter 2:9).

We have established that the bull offering was representative of the priests, being required for their ordination and as their sin offering. But we have not seen two rams sacrificed before. Just like the daily offering is doubled on the Sabbath, the special day of the week, at Aaron's ordination the ram that pictures the substitutionary work of Christ is doubled. This is an extra special occasion as the high priest, who will enter into the very presence of God on behalf of the people, is consecrated. The magnitude of Aaron's calling warrants the doubling of the ram sacrifice.

Now on Pentecost a new priesthood is being established, and it is even more magnificent! Now all God's people have access to his throne, not just the high priest. And not only can they approach the throne of grace, they have God the Spirit dwelling inside them. Such a momentous event calls for the doubling of the ram sacrifice.

A fellowship offering of two lambs was also included on Pentecost. None of the feasts so far have featured a fellowship offering. With Pentecost a new relationship between God and man is established. This pictures the new fellowship between God and man as the Spirit has come to dwell in our hearts. The fact that there are two lambs may point to the two types of people now included in the family of God, both Jew and Gentile. Or the two may symbolize the continuing nature of our sanctification by the Spirit, just like the continuous burning of the two lambs for the daily sacrifice.

Pentecost Sacrifice

Requirement	Meaning
7 lambs burnt offering	Consecration of Gentile church
1 bull burnt offering	Ordination of priests (the church)
2 rams burnt offering	Ordination of priests (the church)
1 goat sin offering	Atonement through blood of Christ
2 lambs fellowship offering	Fellowship with God through indwelling Spirit

    Sticking out like a sore thumb in the regulations about Pentecost is the fact that the two loaves were to have leaven. That's right, leaven, the substance strictly forbidden at Passover and Unleavened Bread. Leaven that represents sin and hypocrisy. Why would God sanction an offering containing leaven?

    God is telling us in advance about the nature of his kingdom. Jesus said his kingdom would be like a lump of dough with leaven worked all through it. He said the kingdom is like a mustard tree that even affords roosts for devilish birds. It is like a field with weeds among the wheat and a fishing net with bad fish mixed in with the good (Matthew 13). Christ's kingdom will not yet be perfect, it will still contain sin.

    And this is what we see at Pentecost. The Spirit comes and indwells the believers, securing their salvation and empowering them to spread the kingdom throughout the world. But those believers are not perfected. They still stumble and fall, they are still encumbered with a sinful nature that entices them away from righteousness. Not only that, there are pretenders among them. There are people who act like followers of Jesus but who are really wolves in sheep's clothing. Jesus said that not all that call him "Lord, Lord" actually belong to him (Matthew 7:22-23). So the two loaves waved at Pentecost are leavened.

Why are there two loaves waved? This is not as immediately obvious, but it seems to picture the two kinds of people who become one in the new kingdom. The apostle Paul explains to the Ephesian church that by the sacrifice of Christ the two types of people, Jew and Gentile, are brought together into one by the Spirit (Ephesians 2:11-18). Therefore, not only Jews, but Gentiles as well, are called into the kingdom and enjoy the blessings of the Spirit and the promises he makes certain. The inclusion of the Gentiles into God's family was a shocking discovery to the early Jewish believers, but it was prophesied all along in the Feast of Pentecost.

The two loaves of Pentecost also contrast with the one sheaf that was waved at Firstfruits. The single sheaf of raw grain that was presented before God at Firstfruits has now multiplied into two loaves that have been harvested, threshed, mixed into dough, and baked. The resurrection of Christ from the dead at Firstfruits has now, at Pentecost, multiplied into the sealing of thousands of believers for resurrection at the last day. And the effects of that momentous day continue to expand as the promise of the Spirit is poured out on all who believe, whether Jew or

Gentile, resulting in the innumerable multitude from every language and nation gathered around God's throne in praise (Revelation 7:9).

Harvesting Practices

Another oddity in the text about this feast is verse 22:

And when you reap the harvest of your land, you shall not reap your field right up to its edge, nor shall you gather the gleanings after your harvest. You shall leave them for the poor and for the sojourner: I am the LORD your God.
Leviticus 23:22

This sounds out of place to our modern ears. God gives the requirements for celebrating a festival and then tacks onto the end an obscure command to be sloppy about harvesting your fields. What about "waste not, want not"? What about being good stewards of what God has given? My mother always told me to clean my plate because there were starving kids in China. Using that logic, I thought about sending the food I didn't like overseas. In this passage, God basically agrees with my childish reasoning as he says, "Don't cut right up to the edges of your property and don't go back to pick up the grain you dropped the first time through the field." Instead, leave it for the poor and the foreigner. Leave it for those starving kids in China.

God commanded this seemingly lazy harvesting technique to be Israel's welfare system. Those with no other means of support could find some food this way. The destitute Moabite, Ruth, took advantage of this system by gleaning in Boaz's field so that she and her mother-in-law,

Naomi, might survive (Ruth 2:3). But what does this have to do with Pentecost?

This festival was a celebration of God's gracious provision of grain. So along with the celebration and thanksgiving for what God has given to us, we are reminded to also give to others. This is how God's blessings always work. He blesses us so that we might bless others. God's gifts are never meant as an end in themselves. He doesn't endow us with material abundance or special spiritual gifts so that we might selfishly enjoy them. God's gifts are given with the intent that we will give to others. Paul says that "to each is given the manifestation of the Spirit for the **common good**" (1 Corinthians 12:7). Peter agrees by saying, "As each has received a gift, use it to **serve one another**" (1 Peter 4:10). Jesus also says that we cannot hoard God's blessings, for if we do not forgive we will not be forgiven (Matthew 6:15). Jesus' rationale is that we have not comprehended the magnitude of what God has done in forgiving our rebellion against his sovereignty if we are subsequently unwilling to forgive the comparatively petty offenses others have committed against us. Likewise, God called his people to demonstrate their gratitude for the harvest by freely sharing that harvest with others.

When we turn to Luke's account of the day of Pentecost we read:

> *And all who believed were together and had all things in common. And they were selling their possessions and belongings and distributing the proceeds to all, as any had need.*
>
> **Acts 2:44-45**

Here in the ultimate fulfillment of the Feast of Pentecost we see the result of the new believers' faith. Just as God had commanded that our thanksgiving for his gifts would be accompanied by generosity toward the needy, the early believers validate the authenticity of their experience by caring for the needs of others.

Pentecost also required a fellowship (or peace) offering of two lambs. Firstfruits had no fellowship offering because it was only the beginning of the harvest. It was not the time yet to sit down and enjoy the fruits of the field and of one's labors. Now at Pentecost it is time to celebrate the crop that has come in, to sit with family and friends and feast on the bounty. That is the idea of the fellowship offering, a joyous feast in the presence of God. And this is fulfilled through the indwelling Holy Spirit. We have fellowship with God himself as we are welcomed into the perfect relationship of the Trinity. It's as if the Father, Son, and Spirit are gathered around the dinner table talking and laughing. And we as believers in Christ are there, too, having his Spirit in our hearts. Because of Pentecost we enjoy fellowship with God, even though we are still imperfect and part of a kingdom that is yet marred with sin (1 John 1:3).

Pentecost Remembers the Giving of the Law

Although the Old Testament does not specify this, Jewish tradition came to associate the Feast of Weeks with the giving of the Law on Mount Sinai. The Israelites arrived in the desert of Sinai in the third month after their deliverance from Egyptian slavery (Exodus 19:1). Then Moses was on the mountain for 40 days receiving the stone tablets. So Pentecost is certainly ***not*** celebrated on the anniversary of the giving of the Law. Still, the traditional understanding was that Pentecost not only celebrated the harvest but also the Law.

With that in mind we recognize some parallels between the testaments. After Moses had been on the mountain for some time the people of Israel became restless and demanded that Aaron produce an idol for them to worship as their god. When Moses saw the revelry taking place at the base of the mountain he threw down and smashed the two stone tablets and destroyed the golden calf. Then he called for his fellow Levites to inflict punishment with the edge of the sword. About 3,000 were killed that day (Exodus 32:28).

Fast forward about 1400 years to a certain Pentecost celebration in the first century A.D. On the feast day that commemorated the Law that was written on two stone tablets all those years before, the Holy Spirit comes and fills a group of believers. Like the zealous Levites who defended God's holiness with the sword, this small group of Jesus' followers goes out proclaiming Christ's victory. They speak in other languages so that the variety of people from all over the world gathered in Jerusalem on that day hear and understand the message clearly. And about 3,000 of them believe and are baptized. In contrast to the 3,000 who died for the sin of idolatry when the Law was given, 3,000 receive new life on this day as the Spirit is poured out. It is just as the apostle Paul writes, "For the letter (of the Law) kills, but the Spirit gives life." (2 Corinthians 3:6)

Luke also reports that on the day of Pentecost the followers of Jesus were all gathered together when

> *suddenly there came from heaven a sound like a mighty rushing wind, and it filled the entire house where they were sitting*
>
> **Acts 2:2**

Traditionally we have assumed the house where the believers were gathered was the same upper room where Jesus ate the last supper with his disciples, or was the place where the disciples hid after the crucifixion, which may or may not have been the same place. But that may not be correct.

Luke says the wind of the Spirit blew through the house where they were sitting. What is that house? The Bible often refers to the temple as a house. Solomon said he had built a *house* for God (1 Kings 8:13) and Jesus drove the moneychangers out of the temple declaring that God's *house* was to be a house of prayer (Matthew 21:13). So the word house could be describing the temple. This fits with everything Luke tells us. He says there were 120 believers gathered together. There were probably not many houses in cramped Jerusalem that could accommodate 120 people. Later Peter says that it was 9:00 in the morning, the time of morning prayer, when the Spirit indwelt the believers. Where would these Jewish followers of Jesus have been gathered together at the time of prayer on a major feast day? Very likely the temple courts. And how was there a great crowd of people nearby to hear the believers speaking in all those languages? Again, it would make sense that they were in the temple courts where the crowds had gathered on this important holiday.

So if the house the believers were sitting in was the temple, then we have a powerful picture of what is taking place on this momentous occasion. The temple was understood to be the dwelling place of God. It was there that God resided, it was there that his people came to meet with him and offer their sacrifices. When the Spirit blows through the temple and comes to rest on the followers of Jesus, God is changing addresses. He no longer resides within the stone walls of a man-made structure. He now lives in his people, the temple that his Son has built.

God had appeared in flaming fire on Mount Sinai when he spoke the Ten Commandments to his people (Exodus 19:18). On this day celebrating the giving of the Law, flames of fire come to rest on the followers of Jesus. The point is unmistakable. The God who dwelt in flaming fire on the mountaintop has moved to a new location, the hearts of his people. Just as the Law came down from Mount Sinai to transform a group of slaves into God's special people, the Spirit has come down from Mount Zion to the followers of a New Moses, transforming them into God's holy people.

Pentecost Represents a Jubilee

But Pentecost pictures even more. God established a 50 year cycle in Israel. Every seventh year was to be a Sabbath when the land was allowed to rest. The Jews were to leave the ground fallow and eat only what grew of itself during that year. All debts were cancelled and slaves were freed as well. Then, after seven Sabbath years, the 50th year was called a Jubilee. It basically was a "super Sabbath" year. In that year all property reverted to its original owner. Everyone returned to his ancestral land regardless of the business transactions of the previous decades. Perhaps an Israelite had fallen on hard times and needed to liquidate his assets. He might be forced to sell his inheritance, the land that had been in his family since Joshua allotted portions to the various tribes after leading them into the Promised Land. But in the Jubilee year he regained his possession. In this way the Lord kept the ancient tribal allotments intact.

Pentecost is the Jubilee year in miniature. Instead of seven Sabbath years it is seven Sabbath weeks that are counted off. Then comes the 50th day, a special Sabbath day. We see the fulfillment of the Jubilee in Pentecost as all rebellious, sinful souls who repent and trust in the blood of Jesus now return to the original Owner. Our debt of sin is cancelled. We, who were enslaved to the Old Covenant Law that condemned us, are now set free with the New Covenant written on our hearts.

And we are called to live out this Jubilee. Jesus instructs us to pray

and forgive us our debts, as we also have forgiven our debtors.
Matthew 6:12

Jesus is talking about forgiveness of sins in this context, yet he chooses to use financial language. The word "debts" is used here instead of sins because Jesus wants us to understand we have entered into a perpetual state of Jubilee. Christ's death has won forgiveness and we as his followers are commissioned to preach that forgiveness and pass it on abundantly. No matter what sin debts may have piled up over the years, Jesus has initiated the Jubilee and those debts are cancelled.

1400 years before Christ, God instituted the four spring feasts in Israel. He very meticulously specified the very days and ways these things were to be celebrated. And Jesus fulfilled them in exactly the right ways and on exactly the right days.

- Jesus, the Passover Lamb, is set apart at his triumphal entry (10th day of the first month)

- Jesus dies at the time of the sacrifice of the Passover lambs (evening of the 14th day of the first month)

- Jesus' death on our behalf makes his righteousness available, symbolized by Unleavened Bread

- Jesus rises on the third day, the Feast of Firstfruits (17th day of the first month)

- Jesus pours out his Spirit on the Feast of Pentecost (50 days later)

Chapter 6: The Events of Unleavened Bread

Passover, Firstfruits, and Pentecost were fulfilled on the very days the feasts were celebrated. Jesus was crucified on Passover as the perfect Lamb. He arose on Firstfruits, the firstborn from the dead. Then on Pentecost he poured out the Holy Spirit on his followers.

Seeing that each of the other spring feasts were fulfilled with specific events leads us to ask if there was a special event that fulfilled the Feast of Unleavened Bread. Some interpreters conclude that Christ's burial in the tomb fulfilled the feast since that is what happened as the calendar changed to the 15th, the first day of Unleavened Bread.

Assuming Christ's burial fulfilled the Feast of Unleavened Bread is an example of backwards theologizing. These commentators simply look at the sequence of events surrounding Jesus' death and decide that laying Jesus' body in the tomb must be what Unleavened Bread predicted since that is what happened between his death on Passover and his resurrection on Firstfruits. But what is there in the celebration of the Feast of Unleavened Bread that anticipates a burial? Why would the feast last seven days if it looked forward to Christ's entombment? Why wouldn't it be just three days? There is nothing in the feast that points us toward Christ's burial.

So Unleavened Bread does not seem to picture the entombment of Jesus' body. Still, because the other spring feasts were all fulfilled on their exact dates, we must ask the question: Was the Feast of Unleavened Bread also fulfilled on the very days of its celebration? Obviously the sanctification pictured by the removal of leaven was achieved by Christ's death on the cross, but what about the seven days of Unleavened Bread?

We have previously said that the seven days of Unleavened Bread symbolize a new creation and a new consecration. Jesus' sacrifice on the cross created a new people. The eight total days of Passover and Unleavened Bread combined to represent the continuing effect of Jesus' sacrifice, a new beginning, a new creation, an eternal sanctification. We also noted that a ritual cleansing period lasted for seven days and Unleavened Bread pictures our consecration. This still seems to fall short of the perfected fulfillment of the other three spring feasts. The other feasts featured very specific events that happened on the specific day of each feast and perfectly fulfilled their purposes. What specific events occurred during the week after Christ's crucifixion that were prophesied by the seven days of Unleavened Bread?

Jesus' body was in the tomb for the first two days of the feast and then he rose on the third day. The Gospels only tell of events occurring on that one day, resurrection day. The Bible seems to be silent about the remaining four days of Unleavened Bread. Were there specific events that took place in that week that the seven days of Unleavened Bread prophesied?

What the Old Testament tells us about Unleavened Bread

We have identified the seven day periods of creation and consecration in the Old Testament, but there is yet another seven day period that attaches to the Feast of Unleavened Bread. The book of Joshua describes events that probably took place during the feast. After 40 years of wandering in the desert the children of Israel crossed the Jordan River into the Promised Land. They celebrated Passover there in the land and the next thing the Scripture describes is the battle of Jericho, when the Hebrews marched around the city for seven days until the walls fell down. This implies that Joshua and his army were encircling the city on each of the seven days of Unleavened Bread.

But would the Israelites walk around Jericho during the Feast of Unleavened Bread? Joshua did this upon specific instruction from God. Would God have had the army encompass the city during the feast? This seems unlikely because God was the one who established the Feast of Unleavened Bread and said the first and last days of the feast were Sabbaths. Why would God have the Israelites break these Sabbaths by walking around Jericho on the first day and then, even worse, annihilating the inhabitants of the city when the walls fell down on the last day of Unleavened Bread? Couldn't God have had the Israelites properly celebrate the feast and then take the city?

Actually there is good reason for the Lord to have the children of Israel march around Jericho during the Feast of Unleavened Bread. Just as the original Passover was followed by the Jews walking out into the desert, this first Passover in the Promised Land is followed by their walking around the walls of Jericho.

Leaven represents sin. The removal of leaven during this feast symbolizes consecration to God. And that is what the Israelites were doing with the Promised Land, they were consecrating it to God. They were to remove the sinful inhabitants of the land just like removing leaven from their bread. This is especially true with Jericho, for everything was devoted to God. The Jews could take no plunder but were to destroy everything and everyone. It was the same picture as the leaven removed from the bread. This is what made Achan's sin of stealing the money and clothes from Jericho so grievous (Joshua 7:1). Israel was supposed to ruthlessly wipe out all of Jericho just like Jesus tells us to pluck out the eye or cut off the hand that causes sin (Matthew 5:29-30). God had warned that anyone eating leaven during the seven days of the feast would be cut off from his people (Exodus 12:15). And that is just what happened to Achan because of his sin.

The New Testament Fulfillment of the Feast of Unleavened Bread

Jesus' sacrifice on the cross paid for sin and made his righteousness available, making it possible for people to be like that unleavened bread, free from sin. But what happened in those seven days after his crucifixion that necessitated the seven day Feast of Unleavened Bread to picture it? Drawing on the battle of Jericho it would seem that Christ was fighting a war during this time that would defeat and remove sin, consecrate his people, and establish his kingdom. But what war was this?

Jesus very pointedly predicted the destruction of Jerusalem. Could the Feast of Unleavened Bread picture this battle? God brought judgment on the city for rejecting its Messiah and removed it completely because a new and different kind of kingdom was being established. But this does not fit the time frames. The fall of Jerusalem does not fit in a seven day period, nor did it happen during the Feast of Unleavened Bread like the fulfillments of all the other spring feasts that happened on the very feast days. It also puts things out of sequence, for Passover, Firstfruits, and Pentecost were all fulfilled in order with the crucifixion, resurrection, and descent of the Spirit. The destruction of Jerusalem happened some 40 years later instead of on the heels of the Passover when Jesus was crucified. The fulfillments of the feasts would be out of order, so the fall of Jerusalem can't be the fulfillment of a war fought during Unleavened Bread.

What war could be happening for seven days after the crucifixion? In Revelation 12 we read of a war in heaven.

> And a great sign appeared in heaven: a woman clothed with the sun, with the moon under her feet, and on her head a crown of twelve stars. She was pregnant and was crying out in birth pains and the agony of giving birth. And another sign appeared in heaven: behold, a great red dragon, with seven heads and ten horns, and on his heads seven diadems. His tail swept down a third of the stars of heaven and cast them to the earth. And the dragon stood before the woman who was about to give birth, so that when she bore her child he might devour it. She gave birth to a male child, one who is to rule all the nations with a rod of iron, but her child was caught up to God and to his throne, and the woman fled into the wilderness, where she has a place prepared by God, in which she is to be nourished for 1,260 days.
>
> Now war arose in heaven, Michael and his angels fighting against the dragon. And the dragon and his angels fought back, but he was defeated and there was no longer any place for them in heaven. And the great dragon was

thrown down, that ancient serpent, who is called the devil and Satan, the deceiver of the whole world—he was thrown down to the earth, and his angels were thrown down with him.

Revelation 12:1-9

The woman is Israel as this recalls the imagery of Joseph's dream where the sun, moon, and stars represent the family of Israel (Genesis 37:9-10). Her child who would rule the nations is Christ. He is caught up to heaven away from the dragon, who is clearly identified as Satan. Then there was war in heaven with the dragon and his angels fighting with Michael and his angels. It is customary to assume that the event described as the child being caught up to heaven is the ascension. But the Greek word translated "caught up" means "to grab or seize by force, with the purpose of removing and/or controlling--to seize, to snatch away, to take away."[7] This word indicates a quick rescue from immediate danger. The snatching or catching up to heaven is what prevents the dragon (Satan) from devouring the child (Christ).

Was Jesus in danger from the devil after his resurrection? Was Satan on the verge of devouring him just before Christ ascended to heaven? Definitely not. Jesus had already died and been raised to life. What could Satan possibly have done to him then? Satan had thrown

---

[7] Johannes P. Louw and Eugene A. Nida, *Greek-English Lexicon of the New Testament Based on Semantic Domains, 2nd Edition*, (New York: United Bible Societies, 1989), p. 221.

everything short of the kitchen sink at Jesus to kill him on the cross. But instead of that being the devil's greatest victory it became his crushing defeat. He did not gain the mastery over Jesus. Rather, Christ was snatched up to heaven out of the devil's grasp. This led to war in heaven that ended with Satan's expulsion. Thus the war in heaven happens immediately after Jesus' death on the cross, just as Unleavened Bread follows immediately after Passover.

A common interpretation of Revelation 12 is that the war in heaven took place in eternity past, some time before God created the world. Some think that it was Satan's being cast down to earth that caused the earth to be "without form and void" (Genesis 1:2). But such an interpretation just rips this passage out of its context. Clearly the child is snatched to heaven at the crucifixion and this leads to the war in heaven. Revelation 12 is recounting events that occurred in the first century with the incarnation and death of the Messiah.

So Jesus died on Passover and this led to the war in heaven that fulfills Unleavened Bread. But what is being consecrated in this war? We saw earlier how the consecration/sanctification period is seven days and how the battle of Jericho was the beginning of the consecration of the Promised Land. What is there in heaven that needs sanctification?

Revelation 12 makes clear that the dragon had to be thrown out of heaven. It may be surprising to some to hear that Satan was in heaven. The book of Job shows us that Satan was allowed to appear before God. He had access to join in when all the angels reported before the Lord. Since Satan was originally a high ranking angel, he had a place in heaven. And God did not immediately banish him from his presence after Satan rebelled.

God did not expel Satan from heaven as soon as he sinned because of his love for people. If the Lord had enforced punishment on the devil for his sin, God's justice would have required him to cast every sinful human being away also. God could not send Satan away for sinning and simultaneously welcome people who had sinned into his presence. Satan, the Accuser (for that is what his name means), would be certain of reminding God of all the sins of his people and thus the reasons that they cannot be allowed in his presence either. But that was before the cross. The death of Christ changed everything. Jesus' death on the cross satisfied God's justice in punishing sin while allowing God to show mercy to sinful humans. Now Satan can be removed.

But why does this erupt into heavenly war? What is being contested in this war? Why can't the Almighty God eject Satan with a simple word?

Again Revelation 12 tells us that the saints are at the center of this skirmish. The victory has to do with the saints overcoming the devil. The battle is over who is allowed in heaven. Satan accuses the saints, pointing out all their sins that would exclude them from God's presence. But the saints now have the secret weapon that guarantees them victory. They overcome the Accuser by the blood of the Lamb that has just been slain on Calvary, and the word of their testimony that they had placed their faith in that atoning work (Revelation 12:11). Now God can graciously admit the saints he loves into heaven while simultaneously maintaining his justice as he casts out Satan. Just as the walls of Jericho came tumbling down on the last day of Unleavened Bread, Satan came tumbling down out of heaven as the ultimate fulfillment of that feast day.

The following chart illustrates the relationship between the battle of Jericho and the war in heaven.

Passover	1st-7th Days of Unleavened Bread	7th Day of Unleavened Bread
Israel observes Passover for the first time in the Promised Land	Israel testifies to their faith by marching around Jericho	The walls of Jericho fall down
Christ dies on the cross as the ultimate fulfillment of Passover	The Old Testament saints testify to their faith in the shed blood of Jesus	Satan is cast down out of heaven

Just as Joshua led the Israelites to observe the Passover and then begin consecrating the Promised Land by marching around Jericho, a new Joshua (Jesus' name in Hebrew) died as the ultimate fulfillment of the Passover and then consecrated a heavenly country.

The Water of Cleansing

In Numbers 19 we read the regulations for the water of cleansing that was used in consecrating someone after being defiled by a dead body. A red heifer was killed and burned outside the camp and then its ashes were scooped up and stored. To prepare the water of cleansing, some of these ashes were placed in a container and clean water was poured on them. Anyone who became unclean through contact with a dead body had to undergo a seven day purification rite. On the third and seventh days this person had to be sprinkled with the water of cleansing.

Because the red heifer was slaughtered and burned outside the camp of Israel, it suggests that this was foreshadowing Christ's death on the cross that also happened outside the camp (Hebrews 13:12). And the fact that the ashes were then used for purification further indicates Jesus' sanctifying work that cleanses us from the power of sin. This leads us to consider the requirement that the water of cleansing be sprinkled on the third and seventh days. Did significant events take place on the third and seventh days of the Feast of Unleavened Bread following our Lord's crucifixion?

On the third day of Unleavened Bread we know that Christ rose from the dead. That evening he breathed on his disciples and said, "Receive the Holy Spirit" (John 20:22). John the Baptist said the One coming after him would baptize with the Holy Spirit (John 1:33). Here Jesus symbolically baptizes the disciples, foreshadowing the pouring out of the Spirit at Pentecost. Breathing the Spirit on the disciples seems to be a sanctifying act comparable to sprinkling the water of cleansing.

Even though the Gospels tell us nothing of that seventh day of the feast, we may infer what happened. Let us review all the pointers that indicate the events that occurred during the feast of Unleavened Bread:

- God commanded the observance of the feasts with explicit instructions. There are reasons behind the details, so there must be a reason that required the Feast of Unleavened Bread to last seven days.

- The other three spring feasts were all fulfilled by specific events on the very days of their celebration. We would expect the Feast of Unleavened Bread to follow this pattern.

- After their first Passover in the Promised Land, the Israelites fought the battle of Jericho. Revelation 12 tells us that after Christ was snatched away from the dragon at the crucifixion, there was war in heaven.

- The walls of Jericho fell on the seventh day the Israelites marched around it, the last day of the Feast of Unleavened Bread. This suggests that Satan likewise was cast out of heaven on the seventh day of the feast.

- An Old Testament consecration period lasted seven days with ritual washings on the third and seventh days. Jesus performed a symbolic ritual washing on his disciples on the night of his resurrection, the third day of the Feast of Unleavened Bread. Again, we guess that heaven also was cleansed of the presence of Satan and his angels on the seventh day of the feast.

Therefore, the seven days of Unleavened Bread prophesied the consecration of God's people. Christ's sacrifice on the cross provided the means for consecration. On the third day, when the Scriptures required a washing, Christ washed his earthly followers by breathing the Spirit on them. Then on the seventh day, when the person being sanctified had to wash again, Michael and his angels cast Satan and his angels out of heaven for good, thus sealing the consecration of heaven and all its inhabitants.

We must admit that this chain of events is not explicitly said to have happened during the Feast of Unleavened Bread. But as we think through all the implications of this line of reasoning, more and more pieces fall into place. The following excursus will deal with the afterlife of the Old Testament faithful and show how this outline of events we have drawn from the feasts helps to explain other portions of the Scriptures.

Excursus: Where did the Old Testament Saints go at Death?

In the last chapter we studied the war in heaven described in Revelation 12. That war centered on the saints as the dragon, Satan, fought to deny them entry into heaven. This interpretation is based on the belief that the Old Testament saints were not in heaven prior to the death of Christ. Now we will consider what the Scriptures teach us about the afterlife for those who lived before the incarnation of Christ on earth.

Biblical Terms used for the Afterlife

Sometimes we fail to properly understand the Scriptures because we assume the wrong meaning for a word. So first we must carefully define the biblical terms.

Heaven and Paradise

Heaven is the abode of God where he sits on his throne (Matthew 5:34). The word **paradise** appears only three times in the Bible with two of them clearly meaning the same as heaven (2 Corinthians 12:4; Revelation 2:7). The other occurrence (Luke 22:43) is only interpreted to be something other than heaven because of *The Apostles' Creed*. Since the creed asserts that Jesus "descended into hell" after dying on the cross, it is assumed that when Jesus tells the thief on the cross that he will be with him in paradise that he must refer to a place different from heaven. But *The Apostles' Creed* is a statement of the Christian faith from the 4th century A.D. It is not part of the Bible but is a summary of basic beliefs drawn from the Scriptures. *The*

Apostles' Creed is not authoritative Scripture. As we have already noted from Revelation 12, Jesus was snatched up to heaven from the cross. Therefore, paradise and heaven would be synonymous.

The Lake of Fire and Gehenna

Revelation 20:15 says that the ***lake of fire*** is the final destination of the wicked who remain in rebellion against God. After the final judgment, the wicked are cast away from God's presence forever into this place of continual burning. Jesus also gives grave warnings against being cast into ***gehenna*** (Luke 12:5). This term was probably drawn from the Valley of Ben Hinnom, a place outside Jerusalem where human sacrifice to other gods had occurred (2 Chronicles 28:3; 33:6). *Gehenna*, with its fiery idolatrous worship, likely is equivalent to the lake of fire. The devil and his demons are also destined for the lake of fire (Revelation 20:10).

So the lake of fire, or gehenna, is where the wicked will spend eternity, while heaven, or paradise, is the eternal home of the righteous. But there are also temporary places.

Sheol, Hades, and Hell

In the Old Testament the Hebrew word ***sheol*** means the place of the dead. It is a rather broad term that can be used figuratively of difficult circumstances in life (Jonah 2:2), but most particularly means the grave where dead bodies are buried. While some interpreters argue that *sheol* only refers to the resting place of a dead body, other texts seem to hint at it being a place for departed souls (Psalm 16:10). What is clear is that both the righteous (Genesis 37:35) and the wicked (Psalm 31:17) are destined for *sheol*.

The Septuagint, the Greek translation of the Old Testament from the third century B.C., regularly uses the word **hades** to translate *sheol*. The New Testament follows this usage as *hades* is the abode of the dead for both the righteous (Acts 2:27) and the wicked (Matthew 11:23). So *sheol* or *hades* is a rather generic term for the place of the dead. The English word **hell** is often used to translate *sheol* and *hades*. Even though it is the most familiar word to English speakers, hell is not a very specific term.

Hades is temporary. Revelation 20:14 tells us that at the final judgment hades will give up all the wicked within it who are not found written in the book of life, and they will be thrown into the lake of fire.

Several times the book of Revelation speaks of "death and hades." This seeming redundancy clarifies that the inhabitants of hades it is referring to do not include any of the righteous. We will see that formerly even the righteous descended to hades, but these righteous still had life. Revelation specifies that it is the *dead* in hades, those wicked ones refusing God's grace, that are thrown into ultimate fiery torment.

The Abyss and Tartarus

While the devil and all his demons will be consigned to the lake of fire for eternity, there also exists a temporary holding place for demonic spirits. The book of Revelation speaks of the **abyss**, a place where Satan is locked up for

1,000 years (Revelation 20:1-2). Demons likewise expected to be cast into the *abyss* (Luke 8:31). Peter also speaks of condemned angels incarcerated until the time of judgment in **Tartarus** (2 Peter 2:4), a proper Greek word for the underworld. Like hades, the abyss or Tartarus is temporary.

Places in the Afterlife	Occupants	Duration
Heaven/Paradise	Righteous	Eternal
Sheol/Hades/Hell	Righteous and Wicked	Temporary
Abyss/Tartarus	Satan and Demons	Temporary
Lake of Fire/ Gehenna	Wicked, Satan, and Demons	Eternal

The Nature of the Old Testament Saints' Existence in the Afterlife

On the Day of Pentecost Peter says,

"Brothers, I may say to you with confidence about the patriarch David that he both died and was buried, and his tomb is with us to this day. Being therefore a prophet, and knowing that God had sworn with an oath to him that he would set one of his descendants on his throne, he foresaw and spoke about the resurrection of the Christ, that he was not abandoned to Hades, nor did his flesh see corruption."

Acts 2:29-31

Peter's argument in his sermon on Pentecost is that David prophetically spoke these words not about himself, but of Christ. Jesus was not abandoned to hades, the place of the dead, nor did his flesh see corruption. By contrast, the text implies that David *was* abandoned to hades and his flesh *did* see corruption. But Peter is not finished. Not only was Jesus not abandoned to hades, nor did he see corruption, Jesus also went to heaven and sat at the right hand of God. But what about David? Peter tells us more.

For David did not ascend into the heavens, but he himself says,
"'The Lord said to my Lord,
'Sit at my right hand, until I make your enemies your footstool.'
Let all the house of Israel therefore know for certain that God has made him both Lord and Christ, this Jesus whom you crucified."
Acts 2:34-36

Peter clearly says that David did not ascend into heaven. So Jesus at his death was not left in hades, his body did not see corruption, and he ascended to heaven. David, on the other hand, was left in hades, saw corruption, and did not ascend to heaven.

Not only did David not go to heaven, Jesus himself seems to suggest in John 3 that no one before him had ascended into heaven.

No one has ascended into heaven except he who descended from heaven, the Son of Man.
John 3:13

The verb "ascended" in this verse is in the Greek perfect tense. This tense signifies an action that has taken place in the past and its effects continue to the present. Therefore, a literal rendering of what verse 13 says is, "No one is in the state of having ascended into heaven." If that is the case, it would suggest that Old Testament saints did not go to heaven, but instead, as Peter says, to hades.

John's Gospel also seems to speak of Old Testament saints in hades. In John 11 Jesus explains the resurrection as he talks with Martha, distraught over her brother's death, and says,

> *I am the resurrection and the life. Whoever believes in me, though he die, yet shall he live, and everyone who lives and believes in me shall never die. Do you believe this?"*
>
> **John 11:25-26**

Now one might assume that Jesus, in saying, *"though he die,"* is talking about physical death. But if that is the case the second part of Jesus' statement does not make sense or is not true. Is Jesus saying that whoever lives and believes in him will never die physically? Obviously not. He is saying whoever lives and believes in him will not go to the place of the dead. Jesus' atoning death will change all of this. So who is it that Jesus refers to when he says, "whoever believes in me, though he die?" This must be the Old Testament saints who believed and are currently dead, meaning currently in the place of the dead, sheol or hades. Although they are there now, Jesus will give them life when he pays for their sins on Calvary. Those that Jesus says live and believe are Jesus' contemporaries and people living after him who will never die, that is, will never go to the place of the dead but go straight to heaven.

Listen to what Jesus says in John 6:

Truly, truly, I say to you, whoever believes has eternal life. I am the bread of life. Your fathers ate the manna in the wilderness, and they died. This is the bread that comes down from heaven, so that one may eat of it and not die. I am the living bread that came down from heaven. If anyone eats of this bread, he will live forever. And the bread that I will give for the life of the world is my flesh.
John 6:47-51

Jesus promises that the one eating the bread of life will not die. He can't be referring to physical death because, of course, believers in Christ still die physically. He means that now that he has come, the real bread from heaven, those who feed on him will not die spiritually or go to the place of the dead. Those Hebrews who trusted in God in the wilderness and were sustained by the manna he provided all died and went to the place of the dead. But now that the true bread from heaven has come, believers will no longer go to the place of the dead. They will not die and go to sheol or hades, but go directly to heaven.

Jesus explains more in John 5:

Truly, truly, I say to you, whoever hears my word and believes him who sent me has eternal life. He does not come into judgment, but has passed from death to life. Truly, truly, I say to you, an hour is coming, and is now

here, when the dead will hear the voice of the Son of God, and those who hear will live.
John 5:24-25

Jesus speaks of two different groups in this passage. The first group consists of any living person who hears the gospel and believes. Salvation is truly a miraculous thing, it saves us from condemnation. On hearing and believing, we pass from death to life.

But there is a second group as well. This group consists of people physically dead. If Jesus is just saying that when the spiritually dead hear his voice they live, it is no different from his previous statement in verse 24. Here he is telling us what will happen to those righteous saints who passed away before Christ came to make atonement for them. This group is the dead, that is, the Old Testament believers. With Christ's crucifixion and death imminent, Jesus says that the time has come for the departed saints to hear his voice and live.

But how does this fit with Matthew 22:32 where Jesus says that God is not the God of the dead, but of the living? The point of his argument in that verse is that Abraham, Isaac, and Jacob are not dead, but are living. Does this contradict what he says in John 5:25?

Actually the two passages mesh perfectly. In Matthew, Jesus answers the Sadducees who did not believe in the resurrection. He says that Abraham, Isaac, and Jacob are spiritually alive. It was obvious that they were physically dead. But because God is their God, the patriarchs have life. In John, Jesus says that those believers who are physically dead, like Abraham, Isaac, and Jacob, will hear his voice and live. They will move into a new state of being alive as a result of the cross. But this cannot be referring to their bodily resurrection because of what Jesus says in the next few verses.

> *Do not marvel at this, for an hour is coming when all who are in the tombs will hear his voice*
> *and come out, those who have done good to the resurrection of life, and those who have done evil to the resurrection of judgment.*
> **John 5:28-29**

Here Jesus speaks of the final bodily resurrection of both the righteous and the wicked at the end of the age. This is the final resurrection at Jesus' second coming. But this is a different event than the calling of the dead to life mentioned in verse 25. Jesus says the time is now, at his first coming as he approaches the cross, that the dead will hear his voice and live.

There are two major changes in store for the Old Testament saints. In the first century, during Christ's first coming, they will hear the voice of the Son of God and will live. The raising of Lazarus from the dead was a powerful illustration of this truth. Then at the consummation of all things, at the second coming, their bodies will be raised to life and the corruptible will take on incorruption (1 Corinthians 15:52-53). So if the Old Testament saints are still awaiting their bodily resurrection at the end of the age, what life did they receive in Jesus' first coming?

Jesus gives us a glimpse into the Old Testament saints' afterlife with the story of Lazarus and the rich man (Luke 16:19-31). Some commentators consider this a parable and not a real description of the afterlife. But the fact that Jesus calls Lazarus and Abraham by name suggests he is speaking of actual people and a real event. Jesus never names anyone in any other parable. But even if the story of the rich man and Lazarus is just a parable, it is still about a real place. Jesus never made up a fantasy world in order to make his point. All of his parables were drawn from real life situations in places like the vineyard, the field, the courtroom, or the marketplace. So we can be confident that Jesus is telling us about a real place in this story.

Abraham, Lazarus, and the rich man are all in the same place as they are able to see each other and communicate. But they are divided from each other by an uncrossable gulf. The rich man is in agony while Abraham and Lazarus are in comfort. So it seems they are all in the place of the dead, but there is a difference in that place for the righteous as opposed to the wicked. God makes a distinction between those who trusted in him and those who didn't, even though they all are in the same basic place. Thus Jesus says that Abraham, Isaac, and Jacob are living. Then, when Jesus dies on the cross paying for the sins of all those believers who had died, they hear his voice and receive life. That is, they move from the place of the dead to heaven where all believers now go immediately upon passing from this life (2 Corinthians 5:6-8).

That the Old Testament believers went to heaven only after the crucifixion agrees with Revelation 20:5 where certain dead participated in the first resurrection (the righteous) and the rest did not. This chapter in Revelation contrasts the first resurrection with the second death. Only the righteous take part in the first resurrection, and only the wicked are subject to the second death. This first resurrection mentioned here cannot be the bodily resurrection at the end of the age. Jesus says that at the end both the righteous and the wicked would be resurrected, the one to life and the other to condemnation. But this first resurrection includes only the righteous. The rest of the dead, the wicked, did not rise until the end. So at Christ's first advent the Old Testament saints received life, that is, they moved from the place of the dead into God's presence in heaven. Then at Christ's second coming, the Old Testament saints, along with all believers, will be raised to life in their new glorified bodies.

What kind of life was it that the deceased saints had before Christ's death on the cross? Luke's account of Jesus' exchange with the Sadducees over the resurrection helps us.

Now he is not God of the dead, but of the living, for all live to him.
Luke 20:38

The last phrase of that verse is important. God, who knows the end from the beginning, knows those who are his. Even those saints who were physically dead and in the place of the dead, still live to him, for he knows who belongs to him and who will be raised to live with him eternally. Jesus' story of the rich man and Lazarus illustrates this reality. The fact that Abraham and Lazarus are named and the rich man is not indicates the different way that God views the righteous and the wicked. The righteous dead are known to God by name, while the wicked have lost identity. In the same way, Jesus speaks of judgment day when some will come calling to him, "Lord, Lord," but he will say to them, "I never knew you" (Matthew 7:23).

That the righteous dead can be in the place of the dead and yet have life is really no different than the way Jesus talks about those who are physically still alive. We pass from death to life by believing in Christ. There is no change of physical space. Even though we still inhabit the same world that we've always lived in, we now have life in heaven. We do not yet experience that life fully, but that does not diminish the fact that we possess that life. Likewise, the Old Testament saints had life even while they were consigned to hades awaiting the payment for their sins on the cross.

The City of Refuge

The cities of refuge illustrate how the Old Testament saints were held in the place of the dead, or sheol, until their redemption at the cross (Numbers 35:6-28). In ancient Israel when a man killed another man he could flee to a city of refuge to avoid being killed by the avenger of blood. The avenger was a close relative to the man killed who was duty bound to kill the murderer and avenge his death. In the city of refuge the assembly would decide the case. If the man was found guilty of murder he would be turned over to the avenger of blood so that he might inflict punishment. But if the man was found innocent he was spared. Still, he had to remain in the city of refuge until the death of the high priest serving at that time.

The death of the high priest was a very odd and arbitrary way to determine the length of the acquitted person's stay in the city of refuge. A set number of years would seem to be a more just and fair arrangement, as opposed to waiting for the demise of the high priest. The person's stay could then, potentially, vary from a very short few weeks, or months, to a lifetime. Some may have died in the city of refuge as the high priest outlived them. But recognizing that the city of refuge foreshadows the afterlife explains this oddity.

The city of refuge was a picture of what happened to the Old Testament saints. At death they fled to the city of refuge, sheol or hades. There they were judged as to whether they were righteous or wicked, based on their faith. The wicked were given over for punishment while the righteous were declared innocent. But those innocents still could not immediately enter heaven. Within the place of the dead, sheol or hades, there was both a place of torment and a place of comfort. The latter Jesus calls Abraham's bosom. We could also call it a city of refuge. The righteous had to remain in the city of refuge until the death of the Great High Priest. Once Jesus, our Great High Priest, died all those in the city of refuge were set free to go home to their heavenly city. The Old Testament saints went to heaven after the cross. The city of refuge is a clear depiction of what happened to all the righteous dead before the time of Christ.

Consider the pivotal scene in Matthew 16 where Jesus asks his disciples who they think he is. Peter boldly declares he is the Christ. Regardless of our interpretation of what the rock is upon which Jesus will build his church, it is clear that the gates of hell, or more accurately hades, will not overcome it. How do the gates of hades stand against Christ's church? Gates are for keeping out or for keeping in. So is the church attacking the gates from outside or from inside?

It does not make sense for the church to be attacking the gates of hades from the outside. Jesus sends his church to the world, to all nations, with the gospel. He does not send the church to hades. What would they be doing there? Who are they trying to save? That would violate other Scriptural teaching that it is appointed for a man to die once and then face judgment (Hebrews 9:27). Jesus sends his disciples to seek and save the lost. Why would they attack a place where eternal destinies have already been determined?

We might try to resolve this by saying that Jesus speaks metaphorically of the gates of hades as representative of Satan's kingdom. Just as Jesus came to bind the strong man, he sends his followers to extend his kingdom into the domain of the devil. But the fact that Jesus says all this in Caesarea Philippi suggests he is speaking quite literally here. Caesarea Philippi was a well known location for pagan worship. Caves there were thought to be the gateway to the underworld. The gods were imagined to retreat to hades each winter. Religious rituals were performed there to bring the gods back in the spring to give a fruitful harvest. Because of this location, it suggests Jesus is very specifically talking about the place of the dead and not just figuratively about Satan's kingdom. So it is not likely that Jesus is suggesting that his church must attack the gates of hades from the outside.

The other possibility is that Jesus says the gates of hades will not be able to hold his church in. One interpretation of "the rock" upon which Jesus builds his church is that it is Peter's confession of Jesus as the Christ. This is supported by Matthew 7:24-27, where Jesus likens the one hearing and obeying his words to the wise man building on the rock. This passage defines "the rock" as believing Jesus, thus confessing him as Lord. So the confession of Jesus as Christ is at least partly what Jesus has in mind here. (I think he also refers to himself as the Rock, but that is all wrapped up in the confession of that truth as well.) Therefore, what Jesus means is that the church (believers) cannot be overcome (held captive) by the gates of hades.

Again in Revelation the risen Christ appeared to John on the island of Patmos.

> *When I saw him, I fell at his feet as though dead. But he laid his right hand on me, saying, "Fear not, I am the first and the last, and the living one. I died, and behold I am alive forevermore, and I have the keys of Death and Hades."*
>
> **Revelation 1:17-18**

Jesus clearly says he has the keys of hades. The context would suggest that he received those keys as a result of his death and resurrection. As holder of the keys, Christ can release or lock up whomever he will. In Revelation 20:1 he uses the keys to lock up Satan. So Jesus says he will build his church on the rock (the confession of Jesus as Christ) and the gates of hades will not overcome it (will not keep it in).

The confession of Jesus as Christ is what distinguishes the faithful, believing dead from the wicked. That testimony of faith, then, is what overcomes the gates of hades and frees the Old Testament faithful. And that is what we read in Revelation 12. After Christ is snatched to heaven out of the grasp of the dragon (Satan), and then Satan is cast out of heaven by Michael, we read of the rejoicing in heaven.

> And I heard a loud voice in heaven, saying, "Now the salvation and the power and the kingdom of our God and the authority of his Christ have come, for the accuser of our brothers has been thrown down, who accuses them day and night before our God. And they have conquered him by the blood of the Lamb and by the word of their testimony, for they loved not their lives even unto death. Therefore, rejoice, O heavens and you who dwell in them! But woe to you, O earth and sea, for the devil has come down to you in great wrath, because he knows that his time is short!"
> **Revelation 12:10-12**

The ones rejoicing in heaven must be those Old Testament saints, for what other believers are there in heaven at this point? But if the Old Testament saints were already in heaven prior to the cross, what is being celebrated? Satan cast out, certainly, but it is only with his casting out that salvation, strength, the kingdom of God, and the power of Christ comes. Could Satan really be withholding all these blessings from saints who are residing in heaven? Would this not make Satan more powerful than God if he can restrain God's kingdom in heaven itself? Rather, it would seem that the casting out of Satan has now allowed the entry of these saints into heaven where they experience the blessings of salvation, strength, the kingdom of God, and the power of Christ.

The Old Testament saints overcame the devil by the word of their testimony (or the confession of Jesus as Christ) and the blood of the Lamb (who had just been slain on the cross). Salvation and entry into heaven comes as a result of Christ's death on the cross.

The Experiences of Enoch and Elijah

But what about Enoch and Elijah? Didn't these Old Testament saints get taken to heaven? Let's look carefully at the texts.

Enoch walked with God, and he was not, for God took him.

Genesis 5:24

This statement is rather ambiguous. Where did God take Enoch? Did he take him to heaven? We are not told that specifically. But the story of Elijah gives more detail.

And as they still went on and talked, behold, chariots of fire and horses of fire separated the two of them. And Elijah went up by a whirlwind into heaven.

2 Kings 2:11

Here we are specifically told that Elijah went up into heaven. Still we must ask, what heaven? The ancients commonly spoke of three different heavens: 1) where the birds fly, 2) where the stars shine, and 3) where God resides. The text could simply mean that Elijah was taken up into the sky, not that he entered into the abode of God. And it seems that witnesses to the event did not assume he went into the third heaven where God lives. The prophets went looking for

Elijah thinking that God might have dropped him off on a mountain or in a valley somewhere (2 Kings 2:16). So it is not a foregone conclusion that Elijah went into the third heaven. Therefore, the Old Testament is inconclusive about where Enoch and Elijah went.

But consider what the New Testament says. Chapter 11 of Hebrews lists many heroes of the faith, including Enoch by name and at least suggesting Elijah by some of the miracles he mentions. At the end of the chapter he says,

> *And all these, though commended through their faith, did not receive what was promised, since God had provided something better for us, that apart from us they should not be made perfect.*
> **Hebrews 11:39**

This passage clearly says that Enoch and Elijah did not receive what was promised. What promise is that? We must read earlier in the chapter to find the answer.

> *But as it is, they desire a better country, that is, a heavenly one. Therefore God is not ashamed to be called their God, for he has prepared for them a city.*
> **Hebrews 11:16**

The promise is of a better country, which is the heavenly city. So the promise they did not receive was the heavenly city. They had to wait until the fullness of time after the death of Christ to finally receive, along with us, their place in heaven. Where the Old Testament was ambiguous the New Testament is crystal clear--Enoch and Elijah did not go to heaven until after the cross of Christ.

Then where did the Old Testament saints go at death? They did not go to heaven, but to the place of the dead called sheol or hades. Within that place the wicked and the righteous were separated from each other, the wicked being in torment and the righteous in comfort. After the death of Christ, the righteous dead were taken to heaven and that is now where anyone who trusts in Jesus immediately goes upon leaving this life.

The Feast of Unleavened Bread recalls the Israelites' hasty exodus from Egyptian slavery when they had no time to let their bread dough rise. Moses led the former captives into freedom during those days of unleavened bread. Likewise, Jesus, the Prophet like Moses, also leads a group of captives into freedom in the ultimate fulfillment of the feast (Psalm 68:18; Ephesians 4:8).

Therefore, we have this sequence of events fulfilling the Feasts of Passover and Unleavened Bread. Jesus died on the cross as the ultimate Passover Lamb and was snatched up to heaven away from the dragon or Satan, who was seeking to devour him. And with him Jesus took all the Old Testament saints. Satan, the Accuser, then made his full out desperate assault on heaven itself in an effort to block those saints from entering. Like a prosecuting attorney, Satan brought up all the sins of the Old Testament believers. But he failed because the saints overcame him by the blood of the Lamb and by the word of their testimony. Since the price for their sins had now been paid at the cross, these saints testified of their faith and were acquitted. So Satan was cast down to earth. Just as Joshua's victory at Jericho established Israel's presence in the Promised Land, Christ won the battle of heaven and cleansed all leaven (sin) from it. Satan can no longer enter the presence of God in heaven. But just as the battle of Jericho was only the beginning of Israel's possession of Canaan, there is much more territory for Christ's kingdom to take. And Satan will fight hard all the way. Thus, the warning to the earth that Satan is cast down.

Chapter 7: The Feast of Trumpets

And the LORD spoke to Moses, saying, "Speak to the people of Israel, saying, In the seventh month, on the first day of the month, you shall observe a day of solemn rest, a memorial proclaimed with blast of trumpets, a holy convocation. You shall not do any ordinary work, and you shall present a food offering to the LORD."

Leviticus 23:23-25

In high school we naturally associated in groups that fit our interests. This could easily be seen around the lunch tables. At one table would be a bunch of guys wearing letterman jackets or sports jerseys—the "jock" table. Usually near that table was one with a group of girls in cheerleader outfits. Over to the side of the cafeteria, at an out of the way table would be a bunch of guys who all had the latest Texas Instruments hand held calculators (I may have just tipped off my age and which group I was part of). At another table would be members of the school band. At the time I didn't know that even within that group there were further sub-groups. Thinking back on it, I see that there were personality types that tended to go with each instrument, and the musical people clustered accordingly.

The character of the instrument also seemed to reflect the character of the musician. For example, the violin is a very classy, refined instrument. It was played by only the most committed musicians, people really serious about their art. The drums are strong and confident and it was usually self-assured kids that gravitated toward playing them. The bass players were all laid back and cool, almost as if dark sunglasses were standard equipment for strumming the instrument. The woodwind section featured the solid core of the band, not flashy, but carrying a large amount of the work. By contrast the horns were brassy, maybe even a little cocky.

     I have heard from some that were part of the musical corps in high school that there was also a "pecking order." I'm told the trumpet players were at the top of that order. They were the extroverts, the ones out front leading the way. Other instruments just played, but the trumpets would sway and "dance" with the music. Thinking back on it, they may have choreographed their movements beyond just blending their music.

     Trumpet players have probably been like this for some time. The trumpet took center stage in ancient Israel, too. In Leviticus 23 God commanded the Israelites to set aside the first day of the seventh month, having a sacred assembly commemorated with trumpet blasts. In Numbers 29:1 we are told it is "a day to sound the trumpets." There really isn't much more said about this feast. So what is it about? What is the point of the Feast of Trumpets?

     Just as the high school musicians took on the character of their instrument, this feast must draw its meaning from the nature of the trumpet since that's really the only information the Scriptures give us. There were various uses for the trumpet in ancient Israel but we can sum it up in two purposes: celebration and preparation.

The Trumpets Call Us to Celebration

     Ancient Israelites did not have calendars stuck to their refrigerators with magnets. Instead, they were dependent upon people who carefully watched the phases of the moon. When they confirmed the arrival of the new moon, the trumpet was blown to announce the beginning of a new month. So the trumpet was sounded on the first day of every month. This was important for the Jews to be certain they were performing their religious duties on the correct days.

But the seventh month was a sort of month of months. The beginning of the other months may have been signaled with the trumpet blast, but they were still regular work days, unless they happened to fall on a weekly Sabbath. By contrast, the first day of the seventh month was a special Sabbath in its own right. It was the start of the seventh or Sabbath month. Just as the seventh day of each week was a Sabbath day and the seventh year was a Sabbath year, God set apart the seventh month as a Sabbath month. While this did not mean the cessation of work for the whole 30 days, this month that held three feasts (Trumpets, Day of Atonement, Tabernacles) did contain more Sabbath days than any other time throughout the year. Some say the trumpet was sounded at least 30 times on that feast day, consecrating the entire month to God. And then trumpets were blown throughout the month as well.

The trumpet is a celebratory instrument. It is loud and joyful. It is perfect for raucous occasions when you want to just make noise for your team or your cause. Even those who can't play a trumpet want to, so they use an air horn just like a trumpet to blast out their exuberance for the home team.

The Feast of Trumpets signaled a time of celebration. The fall harvest of grapes and olives was in full swing. The country could be grateful for God's provision. And the fact that grapes became wine, a celebratory drink, just added to the festive mood.

The first day of the seventh month also celebrated the new year. Today it is commonly called *Rosh Hashanah*, which literally translates as "head of the year." Immediately we might wonder how the first day of the seventh month can be New Year's Day. It is because the Jews' religious calendar began in the spring, in the month of Nisan when Passover was observed on the 14th day of the first month. But the civil year began in the fall. We do this same type of thing. While our calendar year begins on January 1, our school year begins somewhere in August or September, and businesses may decide to have their fiscal year start at any time. So the first day of the seventh month was New Year's Day.

Tradition says that the Feast of Trumpets was the day for celebrating a new king also. No matter when a king acceded to the throne, his formal coronation was held on the first day of the seventh month. It is believed that Psalm 47 was used on such occasions.

> *God has gone up with a shout, the LORD with the sound of a trumpet.*
> *Sing praises to God, sing praises! Sing praises to our King, sing praises!*
> **Psalm 47:5-6**

Israel's king was God's representative on earth. Even though a man sat on the throne, it was understood that the Lord was truly the nation's King. The earthly king was responsible to God and subject to punishment if he should stray from the teachings of the Law (2 Samuel 7:14). As the new king was installed, the people sang praise to God who rules over the earth through the man he has placed on the throne.

The Trumpets Call Us to Preparation

The trumpet was not only for celebration. The fact that the trumpet could be heard from long distances made it ideal for calling attention. It was used to assemble people for worship, to alert a city to danger, and to call an army into battle. Different notes, numbers of blasts and frequencies, or multiple trumpets were used to signal the various messages. Upon hearing the trumpet, everyone would know what they were being called to do and would set about preparing their response.

The trumpet was also more than just a clarion call. The voice of God is likened to the trumpet. Jewish tradition held that the Feast of Trumpets recalled creation when God spoke the world into existence. The giving of the Law, when God's voice boomed from Sinai like a trumpet, is also cited as reason for the feast (Exodus 20:18).

But most pointedly, the feast alerted people to the coming of the Day of Atonement ten days later. They were warned to prepare for judgment within those ten days so that their names would be found written in God's book. Tradition again held that anyone written in that book would receive blessing in the coming year.

The Fulfillment of Trumpets

Since the regulations for the feast are scant we must draw conclusions about its meaning from other sources. The

Old Testament reports a couple of very significant historical events that took place on the Feast of Trumpets.

From the first day of the seventh month they began to offer burnt offerings to the LORD. But the foundation of the temple of the LORD was not yet laid.
Ezra 3:6

Having been captive 70 years in Babylon, the Jews were allowed to return to their country to rebuild the temple that had been destroyed by Nebuchadnezzar's army. After decades with no sacrifices, the people that came back to the land began again to burn offerings to God on the Feast of Trumpets. So Ezra specifies that true worship according to God's commands was re-established at Trumpets. Then, some years later, another significant event took place on this feast day.

So Ezra the priest brought the Law before the assembly, both men and women and all who could understand what they heard, on the first day of the seventh month.
Nehemiah 8:2

The Jews returning from Babylonian exile, over time, rebuilt the temple and the walls of Jerusalem. Once all this work was finished and the people were settled into towns, they gathered again on the Feast of Trumpets to hear Ezra read from the Law of Moses. Therefore, the completion of the work of rebuilding Jerusalem and the temple was celebrated at Trumpets.

Is it coincidence that these two momentous events in the history of Israel very clearly took place on the Feast of Trumpets? Passover looked back to an historical event, but also prophesied a greater deliverance. In the same way, Ezra's and Nehemiah's record of what happened on the Feast of Trumpets also prophesies what the festival anticipates. The feast looks forward to the re-establishment of true worship and the completion of God's city and temple.

The renewal of godly worship and the completion of the work of rebuilding the walls of Jerusalem indicates a time frame for the fulfillment of the feast. The feast signaled the beginning of the Sabbath month so even though it fell on only one day it truly represented a whole season of the year. Thus we can expect the fulfillment of Trumpets to cover a larger time period, rather than simply being completed on one particular day. From Ezra and Nehemiah we can conclude that Trumpets begins with the establishment of true worship and ends with the celebration of rebuilding complete.

So when was it, or will it, be fulfilled? To answer this question we need to carefully consider all the feasts.

Passover and Unleavened Bread are observed as anniversaries of the historical events of the Exodus. Firstfruits and Pentecost are based on the harvest season and are established in relation to the arrival of crops. These first four annual feasts all found their fulfillment in the last year of Jesus' earthly ministry. Passover pictured the crucifixion, Unleavened Bread the righteousness of Christ now conferred on believers, Firstfruits the resurrection, and Pentecost the pouring out of the Holy Spirit. Each of these fulfillments occurred exactly on the corresponding feast day.

But the final three feasts are different. They are not anniversaries founded on historical events, nor are they situated in reference to a natural cycle. This is true even of the Feast of Tabernacles. While Tabernacles became a celebration of the fall harvest, it was not originally set for that purpose but to be a memorial of the Israelites' wilderness wanderings. So these last feasts are just placed in the seventh month by the will of God, not by any historical or seasonal precedent.

Many interpreters have tried to establish the fulfillment of these last three feasts on the corresponding dates just as the first four feasts were perfectly fulfilled on the very days. This is why most people who try to set dates for the second coming of Christ pick times in the fall. They are basing their idea on the fall feasts. But this assumption fails to recognize the differences between the two sets of feasts. Jesus specifically told us that no one would know the day or the hour of his second coming. We must not expect his coming to happen on the date of any particular feast. He will fulfill the substance of these feasts, but not necessarily on their place in the calendar.

The Trumpets are for Celebration

As noted before, Ezra 3 suggests that Trumpets will begin with the re-establishment of true worship. Jesus told the woman at the well that the day was coming when true worship would not be centered on a physical place (either Mount Gerizim in Samaria or Mount Zion in Jerusalem), but would be in spirit and in truth (John 4:21-23). Later, Jesus denounces the worship of the temple saying that it is desolate or empty (Matthew 23:38), meaning that God has abandoned it. He also predicts the temple's total destruction (Matthew 24:2). It seems that Jesus is saying that the place pretending to uphold true worship must be removed in order to truly establish worship in spirit and truth. Tentatively, then, we can say the Feast of Trumpets begins with the destruction of the temple in 70 A.D.

The book of Hebrews is for the New Testament Jewish church what the exilic prophets were to Old Testament Jews in Babylon. The prophets interpreted the times and gave the people hope that the destruction of the temple was not the end of their faith, but was actually God's work and plan. Jeremiah taught that, far from being God's defeat and the end of the people of Judah, the Babylonian exile was God's temporary punishment of his disobedient people and that after 70 years they would be restored. Ezekiel prophesied that God would one day restore his people to an even more glorious future than the best days of the past kingdom. In the same way, the writer of Hebrews encourages his readers that not only will it be alright if the temple gets destroyed, it is actually inevitable. And it is a good thing. That former tabernacle must go.

> *These preparations having thus been made, the priests go regularly into the first section, performing their ritual duties, but into the second only the high priest goes, and he but once a year, and not without taking blood, which he offers for himself and for the unintentional sins of the people. By this the Holy Spirit indicates that the way into the holy places is not yet opened as long as the first section is still standing (which is symbolic for the present age).*
>
> **Hebrews 9:6-9a**

A major theme of the book of Hebrews is that the new covenant instituted by Jesus is far superior to the old covenant established at the time of Moses. The tabernacle, with all its sacrifices and rituals, is just a picture of the realities that come in Christ. This passage tells us that as long as the first section (the holy place of the temple where the priests perform their duties) is standing, the way into the true holy place is not yet opened. In other words, the temple must be destroyed.

Although Christ was proclaimed King of the Jews at his crucifixion (John 19:19) and claimed all authority in heaven and earth before his ascension (Matthew 28:18), when did he officially take his throne?

Jesus promised some of his disciples that they would not die before seeing the Son of Man coming in his kingdom. A week later Peter, James, and John got a peek into the future on the mount of transfiguration as Jesus displayed his heavenly glory. The synoptic Gospels plainly make this connection, that Jesus' promise to the disciples that some would see him coming in his kingdom was fulfilled by the transfiguration. So Christ's kingdom comes along with his glorification, the return of his heavenly splendor.

While Jesus was on trial before the Jewish leaders he told them,

> *But I tell you, from now on you will see the Son of Man seated at the right hand of Power and coming on the clouds of heaven.*
> **Matthew 26:64**

Now Jesus tells these men who reject his claim to be the Messiah, that *they* would see him coming in his glory. So Christ's glorification and enthronement must have occurred within the lifetimes of these first century men, just as Jesus promised that his disciples would not die before seeing the coming kingdom. Therefore, the reality that the transfiguration pointed toward must have come about within a few decades of Christ's crucifixion, within the life spans of the men condemning Jesus to death.

In Luke 19 Jesus tells a parable about a nobleman who took a trip to a far country to be made king. Others opposed his reign and sent a delegation to petition against his installation. Despite their objections, the man became king, and upon his return he had his enemies executed.

The parable was really almost a news report, for this is exactly what happened after the death of Herod the Great. His son, Archelaus, went to Rome to receive the kingdom according to his father's will. The Jews were fed up with the rule of Herod and tried to dissuade Caesar from giving Archelaus the throne. Nevertheless, Herod's son became king and then killed all his opponents when he arrived back in Jerusalem. But Jesus doesn't tell this parable as a history lesson, he makes the point that history will repeat itself. He is that nobleman who is going off to heaven to be made King. He will return and will punish all those who reject his rule.

Another parable in Luke 20 sheds further light on when this takes place. A landowner entrusts his vineyard to a group of tenants and goes off on a long journey. At harvest time he sends a servant to receive the crop. But the tenants beat the servant and throw him out of the vineyard. After several more servants are treated likewise, the owner sends his son, thinking they will respect him. But the wicked tenants kill the son in the hopes of acquiring the vineyard for themselves. When the owner returns, he kills those tenants and gives the vineyard to others. Jesus says this is the fulfillment of the Scripture that states

> *'The stone that the builders rejected has become the cornerstone'? Everyone who falls on that stone will be broken to pieces, and when it falls on anyone, it will crush him.*
> **Luke 20:17-18**

In this parable God the Father owns the vineyard, the kingdom, and rents it to the tenants, the Jews. Those tenants rebuff the servants, the prophets sent by the Owner. Finally, he sends his Son and the Jews kill him. Therefore, God will take the kingdom away from those tenants, the Jews, and give it to others, the Gentiles. Jesus is the rejected Stone that becomes the cornerstone. Once so glorified as the cornerstone, he crushes those who refused him. This is the sad event Jesus prophesied when there would be no stone of the temple left on another.

So the Feast of Trumpets began its fulfillment in 70 A.D. with the destruction of Jerusalem and the end of the Jewish nation. Regardless of when a king took the throne, his coronation took place on the Feast of Trumpets. Likewise, Jesus had won the right to be King at the cross and had acceded to the throne prior to this time, but his coronation as King, having all authority in heaven and on earth, only became official with the judgment on his enemies, the fulfillment of the Feast of Trumpets.

We see this same scenario with King David. As a teenager, David was anointed king by Samuel. But it wasn't until years later after the death of King Saul that David actually took the throne. Once Saul and his family, the other claimants to the throne, were removed, David was installed. Likewise, once the Jewish nation was removed, Jesus took his rightful place on the throne of heaven.

Again we see in the history of Israel that after David was declared king of the twelve united tribes (previously he had been king of just the tribe of Judah) he attacked and conquered Jerusalem (2 Samuel 5:3-7). Jesus follows this same course, being declared King of the Jews at his crucifixion and then conquering the city of Jerusalem in judgment in 70 A.D.

The sacrifice required on the Feast of Trumpets also pictures this move to a new authority. Numbers 29:2-5 states that as part of the observance of the Feast of Trumpets, Israel must sacrifice a burnt offering of one bull, one ram, and seven lambs along with a sin offering of one goat. Notice that this offering is almost identical to the monthly offering with the only difference being the subtraction of one bull. The monthly offering pictured Christ offering himself as substitute (the ram) for all his people, the priestly nation of Israel along with their anointed priests (two bulls) and the Gentile nations called into his church (seven lambs). Jesus offers us all cleansing from sin and fellowship with God through his blood (the goat).

Standard Monthly Offering	Feast of Trumpets Offering
2 Bulls Burnt offering representing Israel and Priests	**1 Bull** Burnt offering representing Israel
1 Ram Burnt offering representing Christ	**1 Ram** Burnt offering representing Christ
7 Lambs Burnt offering representing the Gentile Church	**7 Lambs** Burnt offering representing the Gentile Church
1 Goat Sin offering representing the atoning blood of Christ	**1 Goat** Sin offering representing the atoning blood of Christ

Since the offering on Trumpets simply removes one bull, this implies that either the nation of Israel or the priests are no longer in view. The apostle Paul plainly tells us that with the new covenant God has definitely not abandoned his people (Romans 11:1). And the book of Hebrews clearly says that because of the cross the Old Testament priesthood has been superseded (Hebrews 8:13). So the bull representing the priests has been removed. The old covenant has come to an end with the destruction of the temple. The sacrifice of the Feast of Trumpets prophesied the day when Christ's substitution for his people (the ram) would simply encompass his people from Israel (the bull) and his people from all the other nations (seven lambs). This same collection of sacrifices is found in the other two fall feasts as well. This tells us that the fall feasts predicted a new day when the priesthood would be gone after the ultimate sacrifice was made on the cross.

The Trumpets are for celebration. We celebrate the blessings we receive in Christ: salvation, being heirs of God and co-heirs with Christ, having the Spirit in our hearts, being part of the family of God, the body of Christ, and the temple of the Spirit, etc. We also celebrate Jesus, our King who is seated on his throne, just as ancient Israel celebrated the coronation of their kings on this feast.

The Trumpets are for Preparation

In Nehemiah 8 the Jews celebrate on the first day of the seventh month after the temple and walls of the city are rebuilt. Zerubbabel, Joshua, and Nehemiah had led the building projects that raised the temple and the walls of the city. In the New Testament Jesus comes to build his church, fitting living stones into a spiritual house (1 Peter 2:5). The parallel seems clear. The Old Testament rebuilding of Jerusalem pictures the completion of the heavenly city, the New Jerusalem. Could the conclusion of Trumpets be when all the saved have come into the kingdom? Peter tells us that God delays the end until all that will be saved have come to repentance.

The Lord is not slow to fulfill his promise as some count slowness, but is patient toward you, not wishing that any should perish, but that all should reach repentance. But the day of the Lord will come like a thief, and then the heavens will pass away with a roar, and the heavenly bodies will be burned up and dissolved, and the earth and the works that are done on it will be exposed.
2 Peter 3:9-10

In other words, Christ delays his coming in order to give opportunity for everyone to repent and be saved. Once the last believer enters the kingdom, then the end can come. This fits with the order of the feasts, for Trumpets is followed by the Day of Atonement ten days later. Once the Feast of Trumpets is completely fulfilled the final judgment will take place.

The apostle Paul likewise speaks of the end arriving with a trumpet blast.

For the Lord himself will descend from heaven with a cry of command, with the voice of an archangel, and with the sound of the trumpet of God. And the dead in Christ will rise first.
1 Thessalonians 4:16

Behold! I tell you a mystery. We shall not all sleep, but we shall all be changed, in a moment, in the twinkling of an eye, at the last trumpet. For the trumpet will sound, and the dead will be raised imperishable, and we shall be changed.
1 Corinthians 15:51-52

It is no coincidence that Paul tells us the resurrection comes with the *last* trumpet. When God's time winds down for Jesus to return, the time of Trumpets will be finished. With the last trumpet the Lord descends and the saints are resurrected. The age of the Feast of Trumpets will be done and the Judgment foretold by the Day of Atonement will have arrived.

John, writing in the Revelation, concurs with Peter and Paul. In his vision of the trumpets he reports what he heard with the seventh and final trumpet.

> *Then the seventh angel blew his trumpet, and there were loud voices in heaven, saying, "The kingdom of the world has become the kingdom of our Lord and of his Christ, and he shall reign forever and ever....*
> *The nations raged,*
> > *but your wrath came,*
> > *and the time for the dead to be judged,*
> *and for rewarding your servants, the prophets and saints,*
> > *and those who fear your name,*
> > *both small and great,*
> *and for destroying the destroyers of the earth."*
> **Revelation 11:15, 18**

Again the last trumpet ushers in reward for the righteous and judgment for the wicked.

Revelation pictures this same reality in yet another passage. In Revelation 15:7-8, smoke fills the temple making it impossible for anyone to enter. The Scriptures report this happening on only two other occasions. After the Israelites finished constructing the tabernacle God took up residence there, filling it with smoke and making it impossible for Moses to enter (Exodus 40:34-35). Then, again, when the work was done on Solomon's temple the smoke filled it and prevented the priests from performing their duties inside (1 Kings 8:10-11). Each time God's dwelling place was completed the smoke filled it. So when the smoke fills the temple in Revelation 15, we can infer that God's dwelling place is finished. And that dwelling place is the church, the spiritual temple that Christ has been building. All the saved have been brought in and fitted into their place in God's spiritual house. With the temple being complete and all God's people brought in, Revelation 16 then describes God's wrath that is poured out on all those who rejected his great salvation.

We live during the days prophesied by the Feast of Trumpets. We celebrate Christ our King who is seated on his throne. The gospel is currently being trumpeted to all the world calling people to preparation, that they might be ready for the coming judgment. Peter goes on to warn us to be ready.

Since all these things are thus to be dissolved, what sort of people ought you to be in lives of holiness and godliness, waiting for and hastening the coming of the day of God, because of which the heavens will be set on fire and dissolved, and the heavenly bodies will melt as they burn! But according to his promise we are waiting for new heavens and a new earth in which righteousness dwells.

2 Peter 3:11-13

Peter gives the basic sequence of events. Currently we have the opportunity to accept Christ as Savior and be holy people as we look for the day of God when he will destroy all wickedness with intense heat. Then will come the new heaven and new earth. This is exactly how the feasts outline it. Trumpets is the time for responding to God's call prior to the Day of Atonement when judgment is made. Then the Lord will establish the new heaven and new earth to restore his creation to its original state of perfection.

The Fulfillment of the Feast of Trumpets

The Feast of Trumpets is a prime example of the backwards theologizing that we talked about at the beginning of this book. Instead of studying the feast to learn the pattern that it lays out first, some interpreters just try to force Trumpets into the service of their pre-established ideas.

The basic belief of those holding to a pre-tribulation rapture is that at some unknown time Christ will return and all believers, dead and alive, will be caught up into the air with him. This will remove from the earth all who trust in Christ and usher in the tribulation, a seven year period when the anti-christ, an emissary of the devil, takes control of the world.

Since Jesus will return with a trumpet blast, these interpreters immediately assume that the rapture must be the fulfillment of the Feast of Trumpets. According to their reckoning, the rapture is the next major prophetic event after Pentecost, so it must be what Trumpets is about.

But this pre-tribulational reasoning works in the wrong direction and fails to take note of some very important facts. First of all, it completely ignores the destruction of Jerusalem. Jesus taught that the destruction of Jerusalem was a very significant prophetic event when not one stone would be left upon another (Matthew 24:2). Jesus said Jerusalem would be destroyed and this was fulfilled in 70 A.D. by the Roman General Titus, who leveled the temple. This was a momentous event in Christ's mind, but the pre-tribulationist pays almost no attention to it. The rapture is not the next significant prophetic event after Pentecost.

Further, the only connection these commentators see between the rapture and the Feast of Trumpets is the blowing of a trumpet. There is nothing else about the festival that corresponds with the removal of all believers from the world.

And then the pre-tribulationist has to explain why there are ten days from the Feast of Trumpets to the Day of Atonement. Had God commanded seven days from Trumpets to Atonement it would have fit very nicely into the pre-tribulation time scheme. Christ would have come for his church, fulfilling the Feast of Trumpets and initiating the seven year tribulation. The seven days would have represented the seven years of the tribulation culminating in God's judgment, pictured by the Day of Atonement.

But the Day of Atonement does not come seven days after Trumpets, it is ten days. This forces the pre-tribulationist into all kinds of maneuverings to explain how seven years fulfills ten days.

All of these problems are avoided if we begin with the feasts and move to the future, and not vice versa. We will see in the next chapter how the ten days from Trumpets to the Day of Atonement are representative of the times in which we live. We live in the time of Trumpets. They began sounding in the first century as Christ came in judgment on Jerusalem, a rival claimant to his throne. Once the pretender was done away with, Jesus was officially installed in his rule. As the trumpet is the king of the band, so we live at the head of the class. The saints of old did not receive what was promised because it was reserved for us born in these last days to bring everything to completion (Hebrews 11:39). The Trumpets sound for celebration, for the Lord's great salvation has come and the nations are brought into fellowship with God. But they also sound for preparation, for we must all accept this salvation before the great judgment represented by the Day of Atonement. Once all those whom God foreknows have heard the trumpet call of salvation and accepted their place in his kingdom, the time of Trumpets will be ended and God will pour out his wrath on his rebellious world.

Chapter 8: The Day of Atonement

> *And the LORD spoke to Moses, saying, "Now on the tenth day of this seventh month is the Day of Atonement. It shall be for you a time of holy convocation, and you shall afflict yourselves and present a food offering to the LORD. And you shall not do any work on that very day, for it is a Day of Atonement, to make atonement for you before the LORD your God. For whoever is not afflicted on that very day shall be cut off from his people. And whoever does any work on that very day, that person I will destroy from among his people. You shall not do any work. It is a statute forever throughout your generations in all your dwelling places. It shall be to you a Sabbath of solemn rest, and you shall afflict yourselves. On the ninth day of the month beginning at evening, from evening to evening shall you keep your Sabbath."*
> **Leviticus 23:26-32**

In my life I have had a few brushes with famous people. I was one of about a dozen clergy invited to a brunch meeting with the mayor of St. Louis. The mayor had previously been the chief of police so he bragged that being an old cop he knew a thing or two about donuts. I must say the pastries he served *were* very good. Then there was lunch with the mayor of Geneseo, New York. The mayor and I, as a local pastor, were both honored guests at a senior citizens club. Interestingly, the mayor's wife graduated from the same high school in St. Louis that I did, and we met in an obscure town in western New York.[8] And then there was the time I was in the same small group Bible study with baseball all-star Albert Pujols.

While I was on my best behavior in each of these encounters, if I were to meet the queen of England, it would require even more preparation. Here is just a sampling of the rules for proper etiquette in meeting Her Majesty.

- You must dress well.
- You must stand when the queen enters the room, but there is no need to bow or curtsy.
- Address her as "Your Majesty" upon first meeting, then as "Ma'am" throughout any subsequent conversation.
- Take her hand and lightly shake only if she offers first.
- You must not chew gum, kiss her hand, or turn your back on her.
- Do not wear gloves.
- Do not keep eating after she stops eating.
- Do not talk about private matters. For example, one would never say "Well, Queeny, are you going to choose Charles or William as your successor?"

---

[8] If you are from St. Louis, the obvious question in your mind is, "What high school?" Just to satisfy your curiosity, it was Southwest High School.

And there are many other rules about how you must conduct yourself in the presence of royalty. How much more preparation should there be, then, when entering into the presence of the Almighty God of the universe?

The Biggest Day of the Year

The Day of Atonement is arguably the most important day of the Jewish year. Passover required the lambs to be set apart four days in advance, and to this day there is at least a day of cleaning spent in preparation for the Seder. But that still does not compare to the ten days of preparation for the Day of Atonement. The Feast of Trumpets signals the beginning of what are called the High Holy Days or the Days of Awe, the ten days culminating in the Day of Atonement. It is a time for introspection and repentance, a time to do good deeds in preparation for the judgment that is coming.

Actually, the Day of Atonement is not even a feast. It is the only mandated fast in Scripture. Fasting is a spiritual discipline that comes from the conviction of one's heart. Traditions grew up for observing other fasts, such as a weekly fast day and the fast of *Tisha B'av* that mourns on the anniversary of the destruction of the temple. But none of these fasts are specifically commanded in the Bible.

Yet it is very clear that all Israelites must fast on the Day of Atonement. Three times in Leviticus 23 God commands his people to "afflict" themselves, another way of saying fast. He also warns that the consequence of not fasting on the Day of Atonement is being cut off from God's people.

The Day of Atonement is also very clearly a Sabbath in which no work is to be done, with the punishment for disobedience being destruction. This is unique, for Sabbath days are not fast days. The Sabbath is a day of rest and enjoyment, not of denial. The weekly Sabbath was a day for resting from work and enjoying food and family. The other feast days may have called for a day off from labor, but they also featured eating a meal. Here we have a Sabbath *and* a fast commanded.

This command to fast on a Sabbath highlights the seriousness of what is happening on the Day of Atonement. Atonement means covering and it is all about the covering of sins. Atonement is made on this day for the temple, the priests, and the people. Although the temple was an inanimate object incapable of sinning, it was still marred by contact with sin. Thus it was necessary to make atonement even for the altar and all of the temple furnishings because it stood in the midst of sinful people. Without the covering of sin for the temple on this day, all other sacrifice throughout the year would be impossible. The temple itself had to be holy as well as the priests serving there so that sacrifices offered from that place would be acceptable and pleasing to the Lord. So there was a lot riding on this day.

The Day of Atonement was also the only day anyone ever entered the Most Holy Place. The temple had three major sections. There was the courtyard where the large altar and huge water basin stood. Within the doors of the temple building was the Holy Place containing the seven branched lampstand, the table of consecrated bread, and the altar of incense. Then, behind the curtain, was the Most Holy Place where the ark of the covenant sat. Only Jewish males could come into the courtyard, only priests were allowed into the Holy Place, and only the high priest could enter the Most Holy Place. And he could only enter once a year on the Day of Atonement. This was because the Most Holy Place was where God's presence resided in its fullness.

```
┌─────────────────────┐
│    Most Holy        │
│     Place           │
│                     │
│   Ark of the        │
│   Covenant          │
│                     │
│  Altar of Incense   │
│      Holy           │
│      Place          │
│                     │
│  Lampstand   Table  │
└─────────────────────┘
       Courtyard
       Bronze Basin
    Altar of Burnt Offering
```

Protocol for Entering God's Presence

So how does one enter into the presence of the God of the universe? To meet the queen you would need to put on your best clothes. But that is not what God requires. The high priest takes off his richly ornamented apparel: the ephod of gold, blue, purple, and scarlet; the breastpiece with twelve precious stones representing the twelve tribes of Israel; the blue robe with pomegranates and bells at the hem; and the turban with the pure gold plate engraved with "Holy to the Lord." He wears none of this as he goes to his special encounter with God. Instead, the high priest wears a plain white linen robe. He dons the garb of an ordinary priest. He enters into the presence of God with humility.

The high priest also enters with reverence. He carries with him a censer filled with coals taken from the altar of incense. These coals are for making a smokescreen covering for the ark of the covenant. Like a peasant not daring to look the King in the eyes, the high priest's gaze is obscured by the smoke. He reverently realizes he does not deserve to be there, but is only allowed access by grace.

Moses taught that no one should go to worship the Lord empty-handed (Deuteronomy 16:16). Likewise, the priest takes blood with him into the Most Holy Place. First he takes the blood of a bull to atone for himself and his family so that he might be acceptable for offering sacrifice on behalf of the nation. Then he takes the blood of a goat for the people of Israel and sprinkles it in the Most Holy Place (Leviticus 16).

Everything the high priest does on this day must be exactly right. The priests would meticulously practice the rituals weeks in advance to be sure they did everything according to God's directives. And this was all done in order to point us to the ultimate atonement.

Jesus has Perfectly provided Atonement for Us

Over and over during his earthly ministry Jesus stressed that his kingdom would not be like worldly kingdoms. He enjoyed none of the luxuries we associate with royalty. Instead, he emptied himself and took on the form of a servant (Philippians 2:7-8). Like the high priest removing his rich garments and putting on the simple white linen of the ordinary priest, Christ emptied himself of his heavenly glory and became a man that he might offer the ultimate atoning sacrifice.

Like the Old Testament high priest, Jesus also entered into the Father's presence with reverence. In Gethsemane he was fully submitted to God's will, praying "Not my will, but yours be done" (Matthew 26:39). And Jesus entered with blood, his own blood that was far more precious and powerful than that of any bull or goat (Hebrews 9:12). So Jesus surpassed the Law with a better sacrifice. Unlike the high priest's sacrifice that had to be repeated year after year, Jesus died once for all (Hebrews 9:25-26).

Has Jesus Already Fulfilled the Day of Atonement?

As was discussed in chapter 8, the offering of one bull, one ram, and seven lambs on this day speaks to atonement being accomplished and there being no more need for the priesthood. The book of Hebrews plainly tells us that Jesus entered the Most Holy Place in heaven with his own blood to make atonement for us (Hebrews 9:12). His death on the cross fulfilled what the Day of Atonement portrayed. This fact raises a couple of questions.

The first question is, **Why is there a second feast to picture Christ's sacrifice on the cross?** Jesus was the Passover Lamb that took away the sin of the world. Why is there another feast, the Day of Atonement, that also very clearly pictures Christ's redemptive work on the cross?

Possibly there are two feasts predicting Jesus' death because the cross is so important and pivotal in God's redemption of his fallen world. Joseph told pharaoh that the reason he received the same message in two dreams was that God had firmly decided what would happen (Genesis 41:32). God had decided before the foundation of the world how he would redeem humanity. He emphatically shows what is necessary for the salvation of mankind by giving two pictures of it in the feasts.

Repetition is not uncommon in the Scriptures. Not only does God reiterate important teachings like creation (Genesis 1 and 2), the Ten Commandments (Exodus 20 and Deuteronomy 5), and the life of Jesus (4 Gospels), the basis of Hebrew poetry is parallelism. Hebrew verse is not focused on the rhyming of words, but on a repetition of phrases or concepts. A statement is normally made and then followed by a similar statement repeating the same idea. While the two statements are closely related, they are not identical. Each one highlights a different aspect of the truth expressed or views it from a different angle. That is what happens with the two feasts pointing to the cross.

Passover is a more positive picture of salvation. It focuses on the deliverance of God's people from slavery in Egypt. And it teaches us how Christ's sacrifice delivers us from slavery to sin and death. Meanwhile, the Day of Atonement gives a more negative perspective. Christ had to become sin for us in order to cover our sins and justify us before a holy God.

There is yet another question prompted by the cross of Christ being pictured in advance in two separate feasts.

God carefully placed the feasts in the year in consecutive order. Passover, Unleavened Bread, Firstfruits, and Pentecost perfectly pictured the exact order in which Christ accomplished our redemption with crucifixion, righteousness, resurrection, and the gift of the Spirit. So it seems that the Day of Atonement is out of place. The book of Hebrews tells us that Christ fulfilled the entering into the

Most Holy Place and the sprinkling of blood for our salvation (Hebrews 9:11-12). **If he already did the things pictured by the Day of Atonement, why is it placed sixth in the series of feasts?**

Again we must pay close attention to the details of what God required in the feasts. There were two goats offered on the Day of Atonement. The high priest would cast lots over the two goats. One was designated as for the Lord and the other as the scapegoat.

1. The goat chosen for the Lord was slaughtered, its blood was drained into a bowl, and the high priest took this blood with him into the Most Holy Place. There he sprinkled the blood before the Lord as well as sprinkling the Holy Place and the altar. This atoned for the temple.

2. The other goat was known as the scapegoat. This animal was not killed but was released into the desert, symbolically carrying sins far away. The high priest would confess the sins of the people over the head of this goat, thus placing the sins there to be carried away into the wilderness. This symbolically removed the sin from the people.

Jesus sacrificed his life and sprinkled his blood to make atonement for his temple, the church. This part of the Day of Atonement is fulfilled and done, never to be repeated again. But the second part of the sin offering of that day, the scapegoat, remains. Sin has not been removed from us, we still live in a world plagued by the curse of sin. We await the time when the Day of Atonement will be completely fulfilled, the day that sin is forever carried away, never to be seen again.

In Matthew 25 Jesus describes his coming in glory. He sits in judgment over the nations, separating the righteous and the wicked just as a shepherd separates sheep from goats. The sheep he places on his right and welcomes into his blessed kingdom. But the goats are put on his left and are sent away into eternal torment. Judgment Day will be the fulfillment of the Day of Atonement. All those who have confessed their sins, trusting in the blood of Christ's atoning sacrifice will enter into life. But those who have refused him will be sent away forever just like the sin laden scapegoat.

In Jewish tradition the Feast of Trumpets heralded the High Holy Days or the Days of Awe, the ten day period leading up to the Day of Atonement. It was a warning to the Israelites to be ready. It was thought that God had written names in his book of life on the Feast of Trumpets. Anyone who was not written in the book then had ten days to perform good works that they might be included. Those in the book on the Day of Atonement were assured of prosperity and life for the next year.

We live in those Days of Awe, the time between Trumpets and Atonement. But it is not good works that will get our names written in the book of life. John writes that if we confess our sins he is faithful and just to forgive us our sins (1 John 1:9). The opportunity is still before us to confess our sins to be carried away from us forever. It is time for us to respond to God's call so that we might be found written in the book of life on that final Day of Atonement, Judgment Day when Jesus returns. And how will we be in the book?

Based on whether we confessed our sins that Jesus might remove them from us by his one-time sacrifice.

Ten Days from Trumpets to Atonement

The first four feasts had their fulfillments on the particular days of the feasts. As the Passover lambs were being slaughtered, Christ died on the cross. The day the sheaf was waved on Firstfruits, Jesus rose from the dead. The Pentecost harvest celebration saw a massive spiritual harvest of 3,000 souls. If the Feast of Trumpets began its fulfillment in the first century with the destruction of Jerusalem and the installation of King Jesus on his heavenly throne, what is the significance of the Day of Atonement being ten days later?

A quick survey of ten day periods in the Scriptures is necessary. In 1 Samuel 25, David is running for his life from King Saul. He needs some provisions for his men and seeks help from a man named Nabal whose property he had protected in the past. Nabal refuses to help and David indignantly sets out to destroy him. But Nabal's wife, Abigail, defuses the situation by providing food for David and his men, unbeknownst to Nabal. When Nabal learns what his wife has done his heart fails him and he becomes like a stone, suffering some type of debilitating attack, possibly a stroke. Nabal remains unrepentant and, after ten days, the Lord strikes him dead.

After the Babylonians invaded Judah and destroyed the temple, they left only a small number of people in the land. When Gedaliah, the governor appointed by Babylon, was assassinated, the people were frightened by what reprisals might be coming. So they asked the prophet Jeremiah for direction from the Lord as to what they should do, swearing that they will obey whatever he says (Jeremiah 42-43). After ten days Jeremiah returns with the command from God to remain in the land of Judah and not flee to Egypt. But the people go back on their word and run away to Egypt anyway.

We read the familiar story of Daniel and his three friends, Shadrach, Meshach, and Abednego, in the first chapter of Daniel. The boys have been taken captive by Nebuchadnezzar, king of Babylon, along with many other Israelites. Because they show promise for having intellectual gifts, the foursome is placed in a special training program to prepare them for service to the king. But Daniel does not want to defile himself with the king's rich foods that were sacrificed to idols. He knew that eating this food was tantamount to idolatry. Daniel asked that they be excused from eating at the king's table, but the official in charge said he could not risk having them look weaker than the other boys. So Daniel made a deal with him to try them out on a vegetable and water diet for ten days. After this test period the official could decide what was best. Daniel and his friends proved to be healthier after the ten days and were not forced to eat the idolatrous food.

In Acts 1, Luke tells us that Jesus ascended to heaven after appearing to the disciples over a period of 40 days. Since the resurrection occurred on Firstfruits, and Pentecost is 50 days after that, we know that the disciples were praying in the upper room for ten days prior to the Day of Pentecost.

Then, in the second chapter of Revelation, Christ encourages the church at Smyrna to remain faithful. He says the devil will test some of them by imprisonment and that they would suffer persecution for ten days.

In each of these instances the period of ten days is a test. Nabal failed the test by refusing to repent during his ten days of grace. The remnant of people left in Judah after the Babylonian conquest also failed by running to Egypt instead of trusting God's instruction. Daniel and his friends passed the test, remaining faithful to the Lord. The disciples also passed the test by waiting and praying until the Spirit came upon them on Pentecost. And even though we don't know the outcome, we hope that the church at Smyrna endured and received the crown of life. So ten days have to do with testing. It is the time to decide where you will place your trust, in the Lord or elsewhere.

The story of Isaac and Rebekah further illustrates this time period. In Genesis 24 Abraham sent his servant back to his relatives in Haran in search of a bride for his son, Isaac. The servant met Rebekah at the well and decided God was telling him that she was the one. Abraham's servant gave gifts to Rebekah and her family, proposing marriage to his master's son. Once the agreement was struck that Rebekah would marry Isaac, the servant was anxious to return to Abraham. But Rebekah's family wanted her to remain with them for a while.

*Her brother and her mother said, "Let the young woman remain with us a while, at least **ten days**; after that she may go."*
Genesis 24:55

But Rebekah said she would go with the servant immediately and they set off to return to Abraham and Isaac in the land of Canaan. This pictures what our response should be to the offer of salvation in Christ. Jesus is like Isaac, the Son of the Father who is looking for his bride. The church is like Rebekah, the woman who is asked to give up everything in order to gain a new country and great blessing. Just as Rebekah didn't wait the ten days but responded immediately, we are told that today is the day of salvation (2 Corinthians 6:2). We should not wait but should accept the blessing Christ offers at once.

Unlike the first four feasts whose spot on the calendar was determined by history or harvest cycle, the final three were just clustered into the seventh month. The ten days from the Feast of Trumpets to the Day of Atonement are symbolic. They picture a time of testing when we have the opportunity to choose where we will place our faith. We live in those ten days between Trumpets and Atonement right now. Just as Peter said "that with the Lord one day is as a thousand years, and a thousand years as one day" (2 Peter 3:8), this is an indefinite period of time. The question is, will we be ready when the Son of Man returns in glory? Will we have passed the test of faith when the ten days have expired?

Chapter 9: The Feast of Tabernacles

And the LORD spoke to Moses, saying, "Speak to the people of Israel, saying, On the fifteenth day of this seventh month and for seven days is the Feast of Booths to the LORD. On the first day shall be a holy convocation; you shall not do any ordinary work. For seven days you shall present food offerings to the LORD. On the eighth day you shall hold a holy convocation and present a food offering to the LORD. It is a solemn assembly; you shall not do any ordinary work. These are the appointed feasts of the LORD, which you shall proclaim as times of holy convocation, for presenting to the LORD food offerings, burnt offerings and grain offerings, sacrifices and drink offerings, each on its proper day, besides the LORD's Sabbaths and besides your gifts and besides all your vow offerings and besides all your freewill offerings, which you give to the LORD. On the fifteenth day of the seventh month, when you have gathered in the produce of the land, you shall celebrate the feast of the LORD seven days. On the first day shall be a solemn rest, and on the eighth day shall be a solemn rest. And you shall take on the first day the fruit of splendid trees, branches of palm trees and boughs of leafy trees and willows of the brook, and you shall rejoice before the LORD your God seven days. You shall celebrate it as a feast to the LORD for seven days in the year. It is a statute forever throughout your generations; you shall celebrate it in the seventh month. You shall dwell in booths for seven days. All native Israelites shall dwell in booths, that your generations may know that I made the people of Israel dwell in booths when I brought them out of the land of Egypt: I am the LORD your God."

Leviticus 23:33-43

The seventh and final feast is known as the Feast of Tabernacles or Booths. Both words are translations of the Hebrew word *sukkoth*. You can remember it this way: A Jewish man goes to his rabbi with a problem. He says, "One night I dream I'm a tabernacle, the next night I dream I'm a booth. Night after night it's either tabernacle or booth. What does it all mean?" The rabbi thinks for a moment and then says, "I know what your problem is. You're two tents."

Past Observance of the Feast of Tabernacles

Sukkoth means tents or dwelling places. It refers to the temporary dwellings the Jews were commanded to build and live in during the feast. They were to gather branches and leafy boughs and construct simple outdoor shelters. It was a reminder of the years wandering in the desert when the Israelites lived in tents. But rather than focusing on the difficulties of desert life—the heat, scarcity, and constant moving—Tabernacles celebrates the sweetness of being in communion with God. It symbolized the freedom found in the desert in contrast to the slavery of Egypt. It recalled the protection of the pillar of cloud and the pillar of fire, and the provision of the daily manna, and the water from the Rock.

The Jews celebrated mightily during this feast. Four huge lampstands were placed in the court of women at the temple. These gave light to the dancing and festivities that carried long into the night. Psalms 120 to 134 are called the Psalms of Degrees. A group of Levites would sing each Psalm, then descend one step from the temple, sing the next Psalm and descend another step until they had sung all the songs and moved down the 15 steps from the temple to the outer court. This ritual was done to commemorate the descent of the Spirit to fill Solomon's temple, which happened during the Feast of Tabernacles (2 Chronicles 7:1-2).

Tabernacles began on the 15th day of Tishri, or the full moon of the seventh month. It lasted for eight days with the first and last being special Sabbaths. Throughout this time the Jews would live in their booths.

As part of the celebration an enormous number of sacrifices were offered. On the first day of the feast a burnt offering of thirteen bulls, two rams, and fourteen lambs was sacrificed along with a sin offering of one goat (Numbers 29:13-16). This offering was repeated each of the next six days with the only difference being the reduction of the number of bulls by one each day. Thus, on the second day of the feast twelve bulls were offered along with the two rams, fourteen lambs, and one goat. Then on the third day eleven bulls and on the fourth ten bulls going down to seven bulls being offered on the seventh day of the feast. The eighth and final day of the feast featured the same offering as what was sacrificed on the Feast of Trumpets and the Day of Atonement: a burnt offering of one bull, one ram, and seven lambs and a sin offering of one goat.

Sacrifices on the 8 Days of the Feast of Tabernacles

1st Day	13 Bulls	2 Rams	14 Lambs	1 Goat
2nd Day	12 Bulls	2 Rams	14 Lambs	1 Goat
3rd Day	11 Bulls	2 Rams	14 Lambs	1 Goat
4th Day	10 Bulls	2 Rams	14 Lambs	1 Goat
5th Day	9 Bulls	2 Rams	14 Lambs	1 Goat
6th Day	8 Bulls	2 Rams	14 Lambs	1 Goat
7th Day	7 Bulls	2 Rams	14 Lambs	1 Goat
8th Day	1 Bull	1 Ram	7 Lambs	1 Goat

The Feast of Tabernacles was also called "Ingathering" as it celebrated the fall harvest. Coming at the end of the year, it was Israel's Thanksgiving. But it did not only look back in thanks for the harvest blessings of the past year, it featured enacted prayers for the coming year. In the water drawing ceremony, the high priest would dip water from the Pool of Siloam and then pour it out at the altar, symbolically praying for rain for next year's crops. This was done amidst great rejoicing. The rabbis said, "He that hath not beheld the joy of the drawing of water hath never seen joy in his life."[9]

Present Reality of the Feast of Tabernacles

On the last and greatest day of the feast, a burnt offering of one bull, one ram, and seven lambs along with a sin offering of one goat were sacrificed. This is the same collection as was required on the Feast of Trumpets and on the Day of Atonement. As noted before, this pictured the present reality that the ultimate sacrifice has been made and there is no longer any need for priests to mediate between God and man. Christ's substitutionary sacrifice was pictured in the ram. This sacrifice was for all his people, Jews represented by the bull and Gentiles represented by the seven lambs. The goat illustrated his sacrifice that covered our sins by his blood and opened the way into God's presence.

The Gospel of John says that the Word became flesh and dwelt or "tabernacled" among us (John 1:14). The word John chose to use in this instance is the word for tabernacle. This simple but profound statement serves as the birth narrative in the fourth Gospel. While John does not include descriptions of the angels, shepherds, or wise men at Jesus' nativity like Matthew and Luke, he clearly presents the eternal God becoming a man, the essence of the incarnation.

While we do not know exactly when Jesus was born, a general time frame can be deduced from the narrative of the birth of John the Baptist. The angel Gabriel appeared to

---

[9] Mishnah, Suk. V:1.

Zechariah to announce the birth of his son, John, while Zechariah was serving in the temple. Zechariah was in the priestly division of Abijah (Luke 1:5) and Abijah was eighth in the rotation of priests (1 Chronicles 24:10). Each division of priests would serve two weeks, so that means that Zechariah would have been in the temple sometime during the fifteenth or sixteenth weeks of the year, or around the end of the fourth month. If we assume Zechariah's wife, Elizabeth, became pregnant soon after this, her nine months would bring us back to the first month of the year for a likely birth date for John the Baptist.

Since Jesus was six months younger than John (Luke 1:36), we can then estimate that Jesus would have been born in the seventh month of the year, possibly at the Feast of Tabernacles. This makes logical sense of Luke's birth narrative where the overcrowding forces Mary to have her baby in a stable. Caesar would likely have allowed a time frame to register for the census, possibly a period of several months. Everyone would not have needed to come to Bethlehem at the same time for taxation purposes. But many would have come in conjunction with the Feast of Tabernacles when they were required to appear in Jerusalem. Joseph, and many others, probably were killing two birds with one stone by traveling home to register at the time of the festival.

Although we cannot firmly prove the date, it would be fitting for Christ to be born during this feast that celebrates God tabernacling with his people, for that is what the Lord was accomplishing in his birth. And it would seem especially fitting if the Messiah arrived on the first day of Tabernacles and then was circumcised on the eighth and final day of the feast. It just might be another reason that the feast had to last eight days.

Admittedly, this line of reasoning for the date of the nativity is based on several suppositions and is far from ironclad. But whether or not Jesus was born and/or circumcised during the Feast of Tabernacles, his birth did begin the fulfillment of the festival. In the incarnation God became a man, fulfilling the prophecy of Isaiah that he would be called "Immanuel" or "God with us." So in his earthly ministry Jesus was fulfilling the Feast of Tabernacles since God had come to live with men.

Then in John 14:18 Jesus promised that he would not leave his disciples as orphans but that he would come to them. This is in the context of explaining that he would send the Holy Spirit to indwell the believers. We live in this reality now, where Christ has tabernacled in our hearts. That was the distinctive feature of the Old Testament tabernacle and then the temple, that God dwelt within it. But he no longer inhabits a tent or a building, now he inhabits his people, the church. We are literally the temple of the Holy Spirit (1 Corinthians 3:16). We live in fulfillment of the Feast of Tabernacles.

The Feast of Tabernacles was also the setting for what Jesus did and taught in John 7 and 8. The Scripture says it was the last and greatest day of the feast. It was probably as the water drawing ceremony was taking place, as the priest was pouring out the water and praying for rain in the coming year. Jesus shouted out in the temple courts to all who were thirsty and offered living water that will spring up to eternal life (John 7:37-39). John plainly tells us that this living water is the Spirit. So again Tabernacles is fulfilled in our day.

This feast was the catalyst for Jesus' claim to be the Light of the world, too. The scene was likely while people were in high spirits dancing in the courtyard illuminated by the giant lampstands. Jesus called attention to the blazing lamps and said that he is the Light. Isaiah 49:6 had said the Messiah would be a light for the Gentiles. Zechariah calls all nations to come celebrate the Feast of Tabernacles (Zechariah 14:16-19). By identifying himself as the Light, Jesus showed that the time for Tabernacles to be fulfilled has come. The light is shining among the Gentiles, calling them to come celebrate as part of the people of God.

Interestingly, Tabernacles is the only festival that Gentiles are called to celebrate. This helps us understand the numbers of bulls sacrificed during the feast. A total of 70 bulls were offered on the altar during the first seven days of Tabernacles. Genesis 10 lists 70 nations descending from Noah's sons, so it was commonly assumed that was the total number of nations in the world. Therefore, the 70 bulls of the first seven days represent all the Gentile nations. Just as the nation of Israel was represented by a bull in previous sacrifices, now a bull stands for every nation of the world. Christ consecrates people from every nation, tribe, people, and language and tabernacles with them.

We also notice that on each of the first seven days of Tabernacles there were two rams and fourteen lambs offered on the altar. This is twice the standard amount of one ram and seven lambs from the monthly sacrifice. Just as the daily sacrifice was doubled on the Sabbath, here the monthly sacrifice is doubled in the Sabbath month. The doubling sets apart the seventh month as extra special, but also looks forward to the ultimate Sabbath rest that God will accomplish with the complete fulfillment of all that the Feast of Tabernacles predicts.

Future Hope of the Feast of Tabernacles

Some commentators have interpreted this feast as prophetic of Christ's reign on earth for 1,000 years (Revelation 20:4). But this is another example of the backwards interpretation we mentioned at the beginning of this book. These interpreters have already decided that the Bible teaches there will be a millennial kingdom after the second coming, and they force the Feast of Tabernacles into service to support this teaching. But God gave the feasts first. The feasts should be establishing the doctrine rather than just confirming later prophecies.

Saying that the Feast of Tabernacles pictures the millennial kingdom does not make sense. God outlines his plan of redemption with seven feasts. Tabernacles is the seventh and final feast. Why would the last feast fall short of the consummation of God's redemptive plan? The Bible is clear that following the millennial reign of Christ is the final defeat of Satan and the arrival of the new heaven and new earth. Why would God's great outline of redemption stop short of the ultimate goal, the renewal of all things?

So how do we know what Tabernacles is prophesying? The New Testament does not explicitly tell us as it does for Passover and Pentecost. But the Old Testament does specify a very significant event that took place at Tabernacles.

And all the men of Israel assembled to King Solomon at the feast in the month Ethanim, which is the seventh month.
1 Kings 8:2

Here in 1 Kings we learn that it was at the Feast of Tabernacles that Solomon dedicated the temple to God. They brought the ark of the covenant into the newly constructed temple and the glory of the Lord filled the temple. In other words, God took up residence in this house that Solomon had built. This was in fulfillment of God's promise to David. He had said that David's son would build a temple for his Name.

When your days are fulfilled and you lie down with your fathers, I will raise up your offspring after you, who shall come from your body, and I will establish his kingdom. He shall build a house for my name, and I will establish the throne of his kingdom forever.
2 Samuel 7:12-13

But Solomon's temple is really not the ultimate fulfillment of this prophecy. God says he will establish the son of David's throne forever. Solomon's throne was certainly not eternally set. The kingdom was split in two in the days of Solomon's son, and the throne ceased to exist under the foreign domination of successive world empires. Solomon's kingdom was not established forever.

The real Son of David that this passage refers to is Jesus. He is the One who built a house for God's Name, the church. And his throne is established forever. Solomon and his temple actually just pictured the ultimate Son of David and the temple of the Spirit.

After Solomon completed the temple God descended to dwell in that house among his people on the Feast of Tabernacles. So after Jesus completes building his spiritual house with living stones (1 Peter 2:5), God the Father will descend to dwell with his people. The Feast of Tabernacles prophesies the ultimate goal of God's redemptive plan, the new heaven and the new earth.

> *Then I saw a new heaven and a new earth, for the first heaven and the first earth had passed away, and the sea was no more. And I saw the holy city, new Jerusalem, coming down out of heaven from God, prepared as a bride adorned for her husband. And I heard a loud voice from the throne saying, "Behold, the dwelling place of God is with man. He will dwell with them, and they will be his people, and God himself will be with them as their God.*
> **Revelation 21:1-3**

Three of the seven feasts of Israel were exalted above the others. Passover, Pentecost, and Tabernacles were pilgrimage festivals where every Jewish male was required to travel to Jerusalem. As we consider why these three were emphasized, we can now see that God's nature as the trinity, One God in Three Persons, is the reason. Passover was fulfilled by God the Son dying on a cross. The arrival of God the Spirit fulfilled Pentecost. Now, in fulfillment of Tabernacles, God the Father comes to dwell with man forever. The perfect relation between God and man is restored like the Garden of Eden where God would walk with Adam in the cool of the day. The Feast of Tabernacles pictures the final state of things after sin, death, and the devil have been utterly defeated. God has come to dwell, or tabernacle, with man in his renewed creation.

As we overview the feasts we can also note that the first six feasts are pairs. Passover and Unleavened Bread are very obviously connected. The hasty deliverance from Egypt on the night of Passover led to the Jews escaping with no time to let their bread rise. The names of these two feasts are basically interchangeable, either one can refer to the celebrations of the meal and the whole week following. So it is obvious that Passover and Unleavened Bread are a pair.

The date of Pentecost was totally dependent on Firstfruits. Seven Sabbaths and a day from Firstfruits was Pentecost. The former marked the beginning of harvest and the latter its full arrival. Pentecost is even called a Firstfruits. These two are also a pair.

Trumpets marked the beginning of the seventh month and started the ten day countdown to the Day of Atonement. It was a definite warning and call to repentance in preparation for the one day of the year the high priest entered the Most Holy Place to make atonement for the people. Trumpets couples with the Day of Atonement to make a pair.

But Tabernacles stands alone. It is not matched with another feast nor is its date dependent on another feast. Many have wondered about the significance of Tabernacles falling five days after the Day of Atonement. Some have tried suggesting theories about what future events this prophesies, that there would be a five day gap between the judgment and the fulfillment of Tabernacles. But this is misguided. Tabernacles is not determined as five days after the Day of Atonement, but as starting on the 15th day of the seventh month (called Ethanim or Tishri). The full moon of the seventh month is what marks the beginning of this feast, not the counting of days after Atonement. Possibly God has in mind the "fullness of time." Passover and Tabernacles are the only two feasts established at the full moon. Christ came to earth in the fullness of time and died on Passover, which was always on the full moon. Now, in the fullness of time, when God has determined the end of the world as we know it, the Lord comes to dwell with his people for eternity.

Thus the feasts of Israel can be pictured like the seven-branched lampstand of the tabernacle:

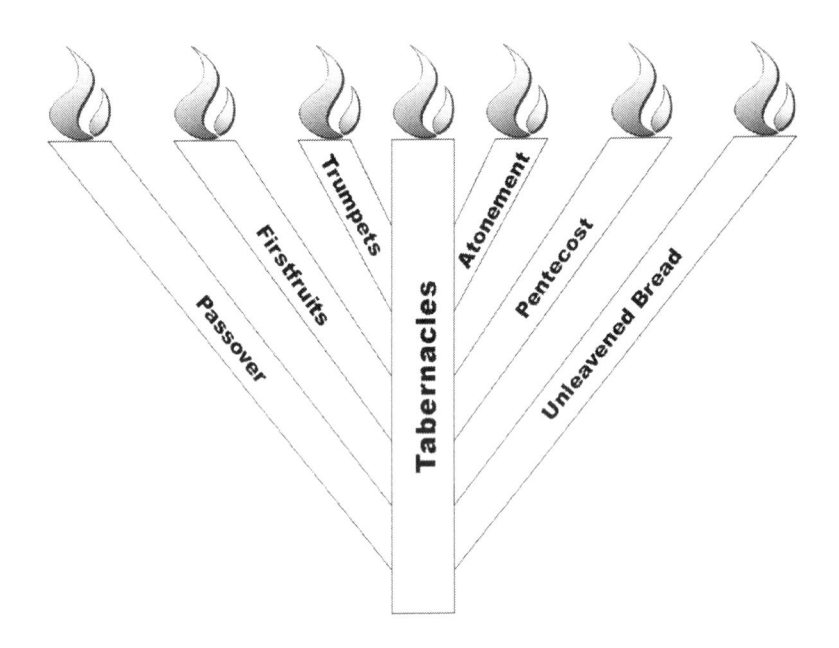

The branches of the lampstand were paired up coming from the same point on the central shaft (Exodus

25:35). Passover and Unleavened Bread are inseparable, coming from the same place on the stem. Likewise, Firstfruits and Pentecost have the same origin point as do Trumpets and the Day of Atonement. Tabernacles stands alone as the center lamp with no partner.

So the outermost branches of our lampstand are completely fulfilled. Jesus died on the cross as the ultimate Passover sacrifice, never again to be repeated. By his death Christ's righteousness is credited to his people, fulfilling the Feast of Unleavened Bread.

The middle pair of branches is also completely fulfilled. Jesus rose again as the Firstfruits from the dead and he poured out his Spirit on the Feast of Pentecost. Christ accomplished all that was predicted by the four outer lamps.

But the three inner lamps are only partially fulfilled. Jesus sits on his glorious throne in heaven in fulfillment of Trumpets, but awaits all enemies being put under his feet. As our great High Priest on the cross, Christ entered the Most Holy Place to offer sacrifice for us as the first goat of the Day of Atonement. But all sin has not been put away from us as symbolized by the second goat.

Even though we enjoy some of the blessings pictured by the Feast of Tabernacles, the total reality has not yet dawned. Tabernacles still looks forward to the day when the dwelling of God is with men (Revelation 21:3), when the river of the water of life is flowing freely down the middle of the New Jerusalem (Revelation 22:1 2), and the glory of the Lord is giving light to all with no need of sun or moon (Revelation 22:5).

We live in a unique time in the history of mankind. We live on the cusp of the age to come. We have the privilege of enjoying some of the blessings of the coming age even now as we live in the old age that is passing away.

- We are a new creation looking for a new heaven and new earth (2 Corinthians 5:17)

- We are ambassadors of a kingdom looking for the defeat of all enemies (2 Corinthians 5:20)

- We are the conduits of living water looking for the river of life (John 7:38)

- We are the light of the world looking for the glory of God to be revealed (Matthew 5:14)

Chapter 10: Already and Not Yet

The seven basic festivals or feasts that God established for his people to observe (Leviticus 23 and Numbers 28-29) easily break into two groups. Four of the feasts occur in the spring and the other three are in the fall. The first four feasts are also tied to historical events or seasonal cycles while the final three are simply placed in the seventh month.

The first four feasts are further intertwined as a group. Passover and Unleavened Bread were established by the historical events of the exodus from Egypt while Firstfruits and Pentecost are connected to the spring harvest. Then Passover and Firstfruits are related to each other in that these are the only two feasts that do not warrant the declaration of a Sabbath in their celebration. Unleavened Bread and Pentecost are distinctive in that both require the standard new moon offering of two bulls, one ram, seven lambs, and one goat, even though neither falls on the new moon. The following table illustrates the interrelationships between these four feasts.

Interrelationships of Spring Feasts	Not a Sabbath	Not a New Moon (but a new moon offering)
Established by the Exodus	Passover	Unleavened Bread
Established by the spring harvest	Firstfruits	Pentecost

The final three feasts all occur within the seventh month of the year and they all feature a specific offering of one bull, one ram, seven lambs, and one goat. These facts tie the final three as a group also.

The importance of these feasts cannot be overstated. God is very specific about when they are to be observed and very particular about how Israel must celebrate them. The reasons for this become apparent when we read the New Testament. The apostles make clear that the first four feasts were prophetic pictures of what Jesus did through his death and resurrection and through the outpouring of his Spirit. Here is an overview of those feasts and their fulfillments:

1. **The Feast of Passover** was fulfilled by the crucifixion as Jesus is the Lamb that takes away the sin of the world (John 1:29)

2. **The Feast of Unleavened Bread** was fulfilled by the righteousness of Christ now being credited to those who believe in him (1 Corinthians 5:7-8) and the consecration of God's people in heaven (Revelation 12:9) and on earth (John 20:22)

3. **The Feast of Firstfruits** was fulfilled by the resurrection as Jesus is the firstfruits from the dead (1 Corinthians 15:20)

4. **The Feast of Weeks or Pentecost** was fulfilled by the coming of the Holy Spirit upon Jesus' followers (Acts 2:1-4)

There is rather wide agreement among Bible scholars on the fulfillment of the first four feasts, but there are a lot of different views on the fulfillment of the last three. Those final three feasts are:

5. **The Feast of Trumpets**

6. **The Day of Atonement**

7. **The Feast of Tabernacles**

The fact that Christians are much more unified and certain of the fulfillments of the first four feasts than the final three feasts suggests that those last three feasts are still pointing toward future events. As we know, hindsight is 20/20. It is much easier to look back at an event and the prophecies predicting it and draw the correlations. It is much more difficult looking forward. Thus, we tend to look down on those people who didn't provide lodging for a couple about to have a baby. They failed to realize that the Messiah was born among them. Yet we have the advantage of perspective and the testimony of those who did connect the dots and see that Jesus fulfilled the prophecies. We would have likely missed it, too, had we lived in Bethlehem at that time.

The first four feasts were fulfilled in the first century. The final three feasts point to things yet to come. This is a very important paradigm for interpreting Scripture. George Eldon Ladd coined the phrase "already and not yet."[10] He saw that there were aspects of salvation and God's revelation

---

[10] George Eldon Ladd, *A Theology of the New Testament*, Eerdmans Publishing Company, 1974.

that were already fulfilled. We already enjoy some of the blessings of his kingdom like salvation and the indwelling Spirit. But there are still promises that we anticipate. We do not yet see face to face nor know as we are known. Ladd taught that the kingdom is both "already and not yet."

The feasts tell us the same thing. We already enjoy the blessings of Passover (justified by Christ's death), Unleavened Bread (sanctified by Christ's righteousness), Firstfruits (the sure hope of glorification guaranteed by Christ's resurrection), and Pentecost (the earnest of the Spirit living within us). But we do not yet have the total victory over sin, nor has our faith become sight, nor does every knee bow to Christ. The feasts show us that we stand in that already and not yet time period between the inauguration of Christ's kingdom and its consummation.

The Basic Math of Prophecy

Bible prophecy can be very confusing. Some prophecies can leave you scratching your head wondering what it was that you just read. You can read it over and over again and still not make heads or tails of it. Our modern day world is so far removed from the language, culture, and historical context of the original writings that we often have no idea how to decipher it.

And then there are all the different interpretations out there. You might read one commentary about a particular prophecy and think you understand that Scripture. You could think that until you read a second commentary. Everything the first one asserted is disproven by the second one, while the author of the first debunks all the theories of the second. It's enough to make you throw up your hands and abandon all hope of ever comprehending any of it.

But sometimes biblical prophecy can be as simple as basic mathematics. A very pivotal equation is

$$4 + 3 = 7$$

What does that simple addition have to do with the Bible? Quite a lot, actually. By dividing the seven feasts into two groups of four and three, Leviticus sets up this basic equation:

4 spring feasts + 3 fall feasts = 7 feasts outlining God's plan of redemption

This is what we like to call "the 4/3 split." There are several instances throughout the Scriptures where a group of seven is very pointedly divided into four and three.

Consider some 4/3 splits in the Bible. In Revelation chapters 6-8, the Lamb (Christ) opens a series of seven seals. These seven seals very obviously break into a group of four seals and another group of three seals. The first four seals are each introduced by one of the four living creatures encircling God's throne and each releases a horse and rider, known as the four horsemen of the apocalypse. The final three seals do not involve any of these: living creature, horse, or rider.

4 seals (with horse and rider) + 3 seals = 7 seals

The very next group of seven in Revelation again very plainly breaks into four and three. The seven trumpets of

Revelation chapters 8-11 are divided into two groups by the designation of the final trumpets as three woes.

4 trumpets + 3 trumpets (or woes) = 7 trumpets

The fact that these groups of seven are plainly broken into four plus three sends us back to God's commands for the feasts. The division of the feasts into four and three holds important implications for how we must interpret the 4/3 splits in the book of Revelation. The feasts offer us the keys to understanding the future.

As we have seen, the four spring feasts were all fulfilled in the final year of Jesus' earthly ministry. The fulfillment of the final three feasts will not be complete until the end of the age. This suggests that the splitting of the seals and trumpets into four and three follows this same pattern. The first four seals and trumpets were fulfilled in the first century in connection with Christ's earthly ministry. The final three seals and trumpets will be fulfilled at his second coming.

This point cannot be overemphasized. Interpreters tend toward seeing the fulfillment of the book of Revelation either in the first century or at the end of time. Some believe that everything John wrote was for the contemporary trials of the seven local churches of Asia Minor that he addressed. They seek to understand the book as descriptive of events occurring in the first century. Others hold that Revelation is all about end time events. They believe we are in the last days and try to correlate the prophecies with what is happening in the news today. The feasts guide us to see that the seals and trumpets are neither all in the past, nor are they all still future events.

Instead, we live between the four and the three. Our justification, sanctification, and glorification are guaranteed by the completed work of Christ, and this is all sealed for us by the indwelling Holy Spirit. The first four feasts have been completely fulfilled.

But the final three feasts are only partially fulfilled. The Feast of Trumpets has begun as we celebrate our King reigning on his throne and as we trumpet the message of the gospel throughout the world, calling all nations to repentance. But the feast is not complete since there are still more to be brought into the kingdom. Jesus has not finished building the New Jerusalem (the church).

Part of the Day of Atonement has been fulfilled as Christ has entered into the Most Holy Place with his own blood, opening the way into God's presence. He has finished the work pictured by the first goat. Yet we still await the fulfillment of the prophecy of the scapegoat. Sin has not been banished from us forever. We still look forward to the removal of the presence of sin.

And we live in the time of Tabernacles. Christ tabernacled among us and has sent his Spirit who currently tabernacles in our hearts. But the new heaven and the new earth is not yet reality. We still wait for the day when our faith will be sight and we will live in a perfectly recreated world in sweet and direct fellowship with Almighty God.

Splitting the Seals

Because of the 4/3 split, we should look for the meaning and fulfillment of the first four seals in the first century. The following is an example of how an understanding of the feasts guides our interpretation of prophetic texts. This is an interpretation of the seven seals of Revelation.

> *Now I watched when the Lamb opened one of the seven seals, and I heard one of the four living creatures say with a voice like thunder, "Come!" And I looked, and behold, a white horse! And its rider had a bow, and a crown was given to him, and he came out conquering, and to conquer.*
>
> **Revelation 6:1-2**

When Jesus opens the first seal in Revelation 6, John sees a rider on a white horse. Many commentators have identified this rider as the anti-christ, but that is an assumption that arises from their predetermined view that Revelation speaks only of future events. In Revelation 19:11 the Rider on the white horse is Jesus. These future oriented interpreters decide the rider on the white horse that appears in chapter 6 must be a counterfeit to the true Rider that arrives in chapter 19. But the only reason anyone could conclude that the rider on the white horse in chapter 6 is other than Christ is due to their preconceived ideas.

Recognizing the 4/3 split, that the first four seals connect to Christ's first advent and the last three to his second, leads to the simple identification of the Rider on the white horse of Revelation 6 as the same Rider of chapter 19. Chapter 6 describes his victorious riding forth from the tomb, his resurrection. Chapter 19 describes his glorious second coming in power.

Of course, we must account for the different details mentioned in each passage. The Rider has one crown on his head in chapter 6 but many crowns in chapter 19. This is the difference between the beginning and the fullness of his reign. The crown he wears in Revelation 6:2 is the *stephanos*, the wreath crown placed on the head of the winner of the games. The many crowns of Revelation 19:12 are *diadems*, the royal crowns of kings. Jesus comes out of the grave having conquered death and so he wears the victor's crown in chapter 6. But he goes out to conquer the world, to rule until all enemies are put under his feet (1 Corinthians 15:25). At his second coming, he has won converts from every nation so he wears many crowns. He is King of kings and Lord of lords. He begins his kingdom wearing one crown, but will go forth to conquer and win many crowns, the rule of all the kingdoms of the world.

The Rider in chapter 6 also carries a bow as opposed to a sword in chapter 19. A bow is a long range weapon as opposed to the sword used in hand-to-hand combat. This bow is the means by which he will conquer. Thus he will fight this battle from a distance, not up close and in person as he was during his incarnation. The bow and arrows he wields are his people (Zechariah 9:13). Jesus will conquer the world through his disciples whom he sends to spread the message of salvation and extend his rule throughout the world (Matthew 28:19-20).

> *When he opened the second seal, I heard the second living creature say, "Come!" And out came another horse, bright red. Its rider was permitted to take peace from the earth, so that men should slay one another, and he was given a great sword.*
> **Revelation 6:3-4**

Jesus warned his disciples that the coming of his kingdom would not mean peace but conflict and persecution (Matthew 10:34). The preaching of Jesus as King and Messiah forces a decision one way or the other. Those who refuse his kingship are dead set against those who accept him. So the opening of the second seal releases a Rider on a red horse that takes peace from the earth. This Rider is the Holy Spirit carrying the Sword of the Spirit, the Word of God (Ephesians 6:17). This seal describes the going forth of the Holy Spirit at Pentecost as He empowers the church to multiply and take more ground for the kingdom.

> *When he opened the third seal, I heard the third living creature say, "Come!" And I looked, and behold, a black horse! And its rider had a pair of scales in his hand. And I heard what seemed to be a voice in the midst of the four living creatures, saying, "A quart of wheat for a denarius, and three quarts of barley for a denarius, and do not harm the oil and wine!"*
>
> **Revelation 6:5-6**

The opening of the third seal describes highly inflated prices for grain. Basically it takes all of a man's daily wage (a denarius) to buy a daily ration of bread. But this is only enough for one, how can a man provide for his family? The first century historian, Josephus, reported that this was the condition during the siege of Jerusalem. That siege reached its climax in the summer of 70 A.D. after the spring grain harvest but before the fall harvest of olives and grapes. The siege restricted the grain harvest, causing a shortage and skyrocketing the prices. But since the city was defeated and sacked in the summer, it did not affect the fruit harvest that came later, thus the oil and wine were unharmed.

God the Son was the Rider on the white horse and God the Spirit was the Rider in the second seal. Now God the Father enters as the Rider on the black horse. The voice belongs to God as he speaks from the midst of the four living creatures who surround his throne (Revelation 4:6). He holds scales in his hand for he is the Judge of all the earth. Like King Belshazzar whom he weighed in the scales and found wanting (Daniel 5:27), God has weighed the deeds of his rebellious people Israel. And just as Belshazzar's reign was brought to an abrupt end, God's judgment here signals Jerusalem's imminent fall.

Why would God the Father ride on a black horse? The Old Testament prophets often spoke of the coming of the Day of the Lord as a day of darkness and trouble (Amos 5:18). The Father shows up in judgment of Israel for rejecting their Messiah and stubbornly refusing his Word through the preaching of the church.

> *When he opened the fourth seal, I heard the voice of the fourth living creature say, "Come!" And I looked, and behold, a pale horse! And its rider's name was Death, and Hades followed him. And they were given authority over a fourth of the earth, to kill with sword and with famine and with pestilence and by wild beasts of the earth.*
> **Revelation 6:7-8**

The fourth living creature around God's throne was like a flying eagle (Revelation 4:7). This eagle-like creature introduces the fourth seal and signifies swift destruction as Moses predicted would come if Israel turned away from the Lord.

> *The LORD will bring a nation against you from far away, from the end of the earth, swooping down like the eagle, a nation whose language you do not understand,*
> **Deuteronomy 28:49**

The description of the destruction of Jerusalem in Revelation 6 is reminiscent of its previous destruction at the hands of the Babylonians. The same four means of death are specified as when Ezekiel prophesied the fall of Jerusalem in the 6th century B.C.: famine, wild beasts, pestilence, and sword.

> *I will send **famine** and **wild beasts** against you, and they will rob you of your children. **Pestilence** and blood shall pass through you, and I will bring the **sword** upon you. I am the LORD; I have spoken."*
> **Ezekiel 5:17**

Death and hades will be the final enemies Christ defeats (Revelation 20:14). But here in the fourth seal they actually do his bidding, bringing about judgment on rebellious Jerusalem and Israel. We do not live in a universe controlled by equally powerful forces, a dark side and a light side. Satan is not an enemy with equivalent strength to match God. No, God is all powerful. Satan is no threat to overpower him. And God can even use Satan's wicked schemes to accomplish his own purposes of judgment and justice.

The first four seals were all fulfilled within the first century as a direct result of Christ's first coming. Now we would expect the final three seals to connect to his second coming.

When he opened the fifth seal, I saw under the altar the souls of those who had been slain for the word of God and for the witness they had borne. They cried out with a loud voice, "O Sovereign Lord, holy and true, how long before you will judge and avenge our blood on those who dwell on the earth?" Then they were each given a white robe and told to rest a little longer, until the number of their fellow servants and their brothers should be complete, who were to be killed as they themselves had been.

Revelation 6:9-11

     The fifth seal signals a change from the previous four in that the living creatures around the throne of God are not mentioned, and there is no rider on a horse released. This indicates a period of time separating the fourth and fifth seals according to the principle of the 4/3 split. The fact that the martyrs are asking how long until they are avenged also suggests some time interval, for had their vengeance come quickly they would not still be crying out for it.

     But how is it that they have not been avenged? Jesus prophesied that the blood of all the Old Testament martyrs from A to Z, from Abel to Zechariah, would be required of this generation (Luke 11:51). That was fulfilled with the judgment on Jerusalem (third and fourth seals). Why are these souls still crying out for vengeance?

     These martyrs seeking justice must have died after the fall of Jerusalem. They are Christians killed since the first century still waiting for justice to be done. Like the blood of Abel crying out from the ground (Genesis 4:10) these cry out. They are under the altar because the blood of the sacrifices was poured out at the base of the altar (Exodus 29:12).

Having seen justice done for all the Old Testament martyrs with the fourth seal, they now ask, "How long before you will judge and avenge *our* blood?" But even though they must wait longer for the avenging of their deaths, they are given white robes of righteousness and are welcomed into God's presence (Revelation 7:9).

These martyrs are told to wait because there are more that must join their ranks. From our perspective it seems crazy that God would delay justice and allow more of his faithful followers to suffer persecution and death at the hands of sinful men. But God has his reasons, one of which is his gracious forbearance so that all his children might be saved (1 Peter 1:9). This does not mean that God doesn't care about the martyrs. We are assured that "Precious in the sight of the LORD is the death of his saints." (Psalm 116:15)

When he opened the sixth seal, I looked, and behold, there was a great earthquake, and the sun became black as sackcloth, the full moon became like blood, and the stars of the sky fell to the earth as the fig tree sheds its winter fruit when shaken by a gale. The sky vanished like a scroll that is being rolled up, and every mountain and island was removed from its place. Then the kings of the earth and the great ones and the generals and the rich and the powerful, and everyone, slave and free, hid themselves in the caves and among the rocks of the mountains, calling to the mountains and rocks, "Fall on us and hide us from the face of him who is seated on the throne, and from the wrath of the Lamb, for the great day of their wrath has come, and who can stand?"
Revelation 6:12-17

The major interpretive question to answer here is, "Do we take these descriptions literally or figuratively?" The sun being turned black would seem to indicate a full solar eclipse. But the moon being turned to blood suggests a lunar eclipse (the earth blocks the sun's rays and the moon has a red appearance). Both of these things happening at the same time is a literal impossibility, since a solar eclipse happens when the moon is between the sun and the earth while a lunar eclipse requires the earth to be between the sun and the moon.

So the 6th seal is probably a figurative rendering of the world altering events of the last days. A great earthquake and every mountain and island removed from its place speaks of political upheaval as all the nations of the world are shaken. This corresponds with Isaiah 34:1-4 where God says he will judge all nations. Sun, moon, and stars can refer to the nation of Israel (Genesis 37:9; Revelation 12:1). John is consistent throughout Revelation in that "stars" always seems to refer to God's servants and not astronomical phenomena (Revelation 1:20). Jesus himself predicted people desperately trying to hide from God's wrath of righteous judgment by calling for rocks and mountains to fall on them (Luke 23:30-31).

The sixth seal teaches us that there will come a day of ultimate justice. The martyrs of the fifth seal cried out for justice against those who had wronged them yet who continued unpunished. They were told to wait until their fellow servants, destined to be killed as they were, had joined them. The stars falling pictures these faithful martyrs. And the terrified people hiding in caves are those wicked ones paying for their sins.

When the Lamb opened the seventh seal, there was silence in heaven for about half an hour.
Revelation 8:1

The seventh and final seal ushers in silence in heaven. Throughout the Scriptures, those coming before God in judgment are rendered silent (Psalm 31:17, 46:10; Zechariah 2:13; Matthew 22:12). There is no defense before the Judge of the universe. All are speechless before Almighty God. Although Job thought he had justice on his side and dared to demand a hearing before the Lord, he had nothing to say once he found himself in God's presence (Job 40:4).

Just like the feasts, the first four seals were fulfilled in the first century as a result of Christ's first coming and the final three await completion at his second coming. This was just a sampling of how the feasts lay a foundation for the future. A full treatment of the seals and trumpets is beyond the scope of this book.

Chapter 11: The Three Harvests

When they persecute you in one town, flee to the next, for truly, I say to you, you will not have gone through all the towns of Israel before the Son of Man comes.
Matthew 10:23

And this gospel of the kingdom will be proclaimed throughout the whole world as a testimony to all nations, and then the end will come.
Matthew 24:14

In these two statements from Matthew Jesus seems to contradict himself. How can the gospel be preached in the whole world and at the same time fall short of reaching all the towns in Israel? Here is an example of how the framework of the biblical feasts gives us the basis for understanding other passages.

The Jewish feasts were based in an agrarian setting. Therefore, the feasts are closely connected with the growing of crops. There were three principle harvest times in ancient Israel and we see celebrations corresponding to each of these harvests. The barley harvest occurred in early spring and was acknowledged with the Feast of Firstfruits. When the wheat ripened near the end of spring or start of summer it was commemorated at the Feast of Weeks or Pentecost. Finally, the fall harvest of olives and grapes was celebrated with a tremendous outpouring of joy at the Feast of Tabernacles.

Unlike their neighbors who performed religious acts and sacrifices in the hopes of pleasing their gods to insure a plentiful harvest, Israel's feasts were all in response to the gracious acts of God. Because God gave the early barley harvest they brought the firstfruits of that harvest to wave before the Lord. Then when the wheat came in they waved the two loaves of bread at Pentecost. Tabernacles capped off the year in thanksgiving for the full harvest God had granted. Each feast was an act of thanksgiving for what God had provided, not a ritual to coax divine blessing.

But the feasts were not simply rooted in the annual growing cycle. The feasts both looked back in gratitude for what God had given and forward in anticipation, picturing God's redemptive program for his rebellious world. The Feast of Firstfruits was prophetically fulfilled by the resurrection of Jesus, opening the way of salvation to all who believe, including all those Old Testament saints that passed on before Christ's birth. The Spirit indwelt those believers on Pentecost and a great harvest of 3,000 souls was brought into the kingdom. The Feast of Tabernacles is also referred to as the Feast of Ingathering. It anticipates a great harvest at the end of the age described in the book of Revelation. The three harvest festivals prophesy three harvests of souls.

We have established that the first four feasts all saw their fulfillment in the first century through Christ's incarnation. Since the first four feasts included celebrations for the first two harvests, we can expect that the eschatological fulfillment of those harvests has happened as well. The final harvest would occur at the end of the world.

Matthew chapter 10 relates Jesus' instructions to his disciples as he sends them out to preach. A quick reading of this chapter yields some questions about statements Jesus makes that don't seem to fit. We have already pointed out the disparity of the gospel going into all the world and yet missing some Israelite cities. Another question is raised in Matthew 10:5, where Jesus restricts the disciples from going to the Samaritans or the Gentiles, then in Matthew 28:19 he explicitly sends them to all nations. To whom, then, is the gospel to be preached, Jews only or Gentiles, too?

The reason for these discrepancies is easily answered by the different harvests. Just as the Jewish year featured three harvests and their corresponding celebrations, God's redemptive plan features three harvests of souls. The first harvest occurred during Jesus' ministry on earth, the second ran from Pentecost to the destruction of Jerusalem, and the last harvest is ongoing until the second coming. Matthew 10 actually outlines all three harvests and shows the differences between them. Jesus gives a mission, a message, and a method specific to each harvest.

	The Early Harvest	The Second Harvest	The Later Harvest
Mission	To Jews only	To Jews first, then to Gentiles	To all nations
Message	The Kingdom of heaven is near	Speak what the Holy Spirit tells you	Shout what Jesus tells you in the dark
Method	Take no bag or money	Endure persecution	Be Jesus' representative

The Early Harvest

In Matthew 10:5-16 Jesus speaks to his disciples specifically for the immediate moment as he sends them out ahead of himself. Jesus instructs the disciples to do exactly as he has been doing in his ministry. They are sent only to the lost sheep of Israel just as Jesus was (Matthew 15:24). They receive authority to heal and cast out demons just as Jesus has been doing. They are to preach that the kingdom of heaven is near, the same message Jesus preached (Matthew 4:17). They take nothing along on their journey just as Jesus came into this world with nothing. These are the special instructions for the disciples especially applicable to their present mission during the ministry of Jesus.

So the mission of the early harvest was to Israel only, not Samaria or the Gentiles. The message was that the kingdom was near, the same as both John the Baptist and Jesus. And the method was to follow the same itinerant program as Jesus without bag or money.

The Second Harvest

At verse 17 of Matthew 10 we see a shift. All of a sudden Jesus begins to warn the disciples about the opposition they will face. He predicts they will be dragged before councils, flogged in synagogues, and put on trial before Gentiles. We see no report in the gospels of such opposition to the disciples' preaching while Christ was on earth. But this is exactly what happened to the disciples after Jesus' ascension. The book of Acts tells of their trials and church tradition attests that all but John died violently for their faith. Notice also that under these circumstances Jesus promises the Spirit will give them the words to say.

Previously, Jesus gave them authority to heal diseases and exorcise demons. Now they have the Holy Spirit. So this segment of Jesus' instruction is specific to the time after Pentecost.

Then verse 23 says that they will "not finish going through the cities of Israel before the Son of Man comes." So this time period has an end and it must be different from the state of things at the second coming because that will not happen until the gospel has gone into all the world. So what is this coming of the Son of Man that will happen before the disciples finish going through the cities of Israel?

The prophets warned about the "day of the Lord." This term was used for several catastrophic events in the Old Testament. Isaiah called God's judgment on Babylon the day of the Lord (Isaiah 13:6). Jeremiah and Ezekiel spoke of the defeat of Egypt and other nations allied with her as the day of the Lord (Jeremiah 46:10; Ezekiel 30:3). Joel's locust plague on Judah (Joel 2:1) and Amos' prediction of exile for Israel (Amos 5:18) were also called the day of the Lord. So this phrase could refer to any of these events where God brings a disastrous judgment on a sinful people.

But the prophets also spoke of a larger day of the Lord coming in the future. The days of the Lord, the judgments the Old Testament prophets predicted at different times in history, are really just a foretaste of the final day of the Lord when he will judge all rebellion within his creation. The book of Revelation picks up on the various Old Testament days of the Lord and uses their imagery to picture the end of this age.

Zephaniah called for silence on the day of the Lord (Zephaniah 1:7) and the opening of the last seal in Revelation 8 brings silence in heaven (Revelation 8:1). The locust swarm of Joel 1:4 returns with the blowing of the fifth trumpet in Revelation 9:3. Amos spoke of the day being darkness (Amos 5:18) and Revelation predicts darkness in chapters 6, 8, and 16. Isaiah 21:9 predicted the fall of Babylon and Revelation 18 describes the utter destruction of Babylon the Great. Jeremiah called Egypt's defeat at the battle of Carchemish on the Euphrates River the day of the Lord (Jeremiah 46:10) and Revelation 9:14 and 16:12 mention the Euphrates in connection with the final battle. Ezekiel pronounces judgment on the false prophets (Ezekiel 13:2) and Revelation 19:20 tells of the demise of the false prophet and all who believe him. And finally, Ezekiel chapters 25-30 and Obadiah 15 predict the destruction of the nations by the sword just as John tells of his vision of the Rider on the white horse slaying the nations with the sword of his mouth in Revelation 19.

Therefore, the term the "day of the Lord" can refer to divine judgment on a particular city or people and it can describe the final judgment at the end of the world. In the New Testament the phrase "the coming of the Son of Man" and similar statements are used in the same way. They may refer to Christ's judgment on a particular city or people as well as to his second coming in glory when he will defeat every enemy.

We find an example of a coming of Christ separate from his coming at the end of the world in Luke 17:30-33. In that passage, Jesus speaks of "the day the Son of Man will be revealed." Jesus warns anyone on the roof not to go into the house for anything and anyone in the field not to go back for anything. These warnings make absolutely no sense if we are talking about Christ's coming at the end of the world. What difference will it make if someone tries to get something out of the house at this point? All mankind will be judged and it won't matter if they are on the roof, in the field, or running far away. There won't be any escape from the final judgment. So Jesus must be talking about a different and smaller judgment in these verses, a judgment that those who listen to his teachings can avoid by heeding this warning.

Returning to the question at hand, in Matthew 10:23 Jesus must not be talking about his second coming because the gospel will be preached in all the world before he comes. Jesus' coming in this passage is a coming in judgment when he tells his disciples they will not finish going over the towns of Israel before his arrival. When did he come in judgment? He predicted that no stone of the temple would be left on another (Matthew 24:2). This happened in the year 70 A.D. when Titus led the Roman army to put an end to the Jewish rebellion. Just as Babylon's destruction of Jerusalem in the 6th century B.C. was God's judgment on his sinful people, the Romans were Christ's instrument of punishment on the rebellious city of Jerusalem that stubbornly refused to turn to him. Just like the Old Testament prophets spoke of "the day of Lord" coming as destruction for particular cities, Jesus predicts the destruction of Jerusalem. This is clearly a pivotal event in Jesus' mind. So Jesus was telling his disciples that they would not finish going through all the cities of Israel before the Romans would come and destroy the country.

Therefore, the second harvest is a time extending from Pentecost to the destruction of Jerusalem, which is the coming of the Son of Man in judgment. The mission of the second harvest is no longer exclusively to Jews, but includes Gentiles, too. The message now comes directly from the indwelling Holy Spirit. And the method is for Christ's followers to continually preach despite the persecution they must endure.

The Early and Second Harvests in Luke

The Gospel of Luke concurs with Matthew and explicitly divides the early and second harvests. Consider this odd statement Jesus makes on his way to the Garden of Gethsemane.

> And he said to them, "When I sent you out with no moneybag or knapsack or sandals, did you lack?" They said, "Nothing." He said to them, "But now let the one who has a moneybag take it, and likewise a knapsack. And let the one who has no sword sell his cloak and buy one. For I tell you that this Scripture must be fulfilled in me: 'And he was numbered with the transgressors.' For what is written about me has its fulfillment." And they said, "Look, Lord, here are two swords." And he said to them, "It is enough."
>
> **Luke 22:35-38**

Jesus instructs his disciples to arm themselves with swords in this passage. But he can't literally be telling them to take up arms for several reasons. First of all, this would not fit with the bulk of Jesus' mission and message. He consistently refused military action even though many around him were ready for such and pushed him toward it. If Jesus was suggesting violent attacks by his disciples, it also makes no sense that he would say two swords was sufficient for eleven men to topple not only the Jewish authorities, but the massive Roman Empire as well. A short time later, Jesus chastises Peter for using one of these swords in trying to cut off the head of one of Jesus' captors. To Pilate, Jesus confesses that his kingdom is not from this world and that is why his disciples do not fight. Finally, from the cross Jesus rejects the option of calling thousands of angels to his defense. Obviously, Jesus' intention was *not* for his disciples to engage in combat with swords.

So what is Jesus saying here? He first asks the disciples to recall their experience when he sent them out to preach (Matthew 10:5-16; Luke 9:1-5). Despite carrying no money or provisions, they lacked nothing. But now Jesus' instructions have changed. Now they are to take up these necessities. Times have changed. With Christ's impending crucifixion there is a shift in how the disciples must carry out their mission. Jesus is telling the disciples that they are entering a new phase in ministry. Formerly it was the early harvest, but now they are beginning the second harvest.

The opposition the disciples face in each harvest is very different. When Jesus sent them out the first time the opposition to their message was simple rejection. Upon entering a house, if they were not accepted, they were to move on from there. A town that refused their message was left behind with a shake of the dust from the preacher's feet (Matthew 10:14).

But in the second harvest the opposition ramps up. Now the disciples can expect open hostilities: family members pitted against one another, examinations before councils, beatings in synagogues. Previously the disciples could depend upon the hospitality of their fellow countrymen to care for their needs. Now they must carry their supplies with them for they will not find so many willing hosts. Before those who rejected the message just turned away and the disciples were free to move on. Now the preaching of Christ brings not peace, but a sword. This is what Jesus is saying to his followers. He advises obtaining a sword not because he wants his disciples to hack up their enemies, but to make the point that they will face violent opposition. And they must be prepared even to die, just like their Master is about to.

Therefore, what Jesus says to the disciples in Luke 22 is that they are soon to face violence for his name. Just as the Lord provided for their needs in their prior preaching tour, they can be certain he will care for them still. But the disciples in typical fashion misunderstand Jesus' point. Just as they thought of literal yeast when Jesus warned of the leaven of the Pharisees, they think he is telling them to get metal weapons. When they produce two swords Jesus responds, "That is enough." He is saying, "Enough of worrying about weapons, that is not what I meant. But I don't have time to explain it all right now."

While Jesus' full intention may have been obscure to his followers, what is very clear is that he is contrasting the way things were in the disciples' preaching tour during his ministry with the way things will be now that the cross is just a day away. Jesus plainly says that the realities of the second harvest will be quite different from the early harvest.

The Later Harvest

In Matthew 10:26 we read "There is nothing concealed that will not be disclosed, or hidden that will not be made known." What is concealed that will be disclosed?

To whom will the hidden be made known? A comparison with the parallel passages in both Mark and Luke shows that each of the other gospel writers places this statement in the context with the image of a lamp on its stand shining on all in the house (Mark 4:21-22; Luke 8:16-17). So what is being disclosed and made known is the gospel and it is going out to everyone. This is the first indication that we are now speaking of a time when there is no distinction made between peoples, whether Jew or Gentile. The early harvest was exclusively for Jews, the second harvest was to the Jew first and then to the Gentile. But now the disclosure is for all in the house, for everyone everywhere.

The message of the later harvest is what Jesus tells in the dark and whispers in the ear that must be brought into the light and shouted from the rooftops. It is a message that will divide families and that demands total sacrifice.

Jesus goes on to pronounce blessing in verses 40-42 on those treating his followers well, for in so doing they are treating Christ the same way. This matches how Jesus says he will judge the nations upon his return in glory (Matthew 25). So this section, from verse 24 to verse 42, is talking about the last harvest when the gospel is preached to all nations. This harvest differs slightly from the second harvest in that there is no longer any special attention paid to Israel, all nations are alike. Until the destruction of Jerusalem, which was God's final judgment on his rebellious people, the kingdom was preached with preference given to Israel (to the Jew first) in hopes that they would see the error of their ways and repent, accepting their Messiah, Jesus. But once the nation of Israel ceased to exist, ethnic Jews became just like all the other nations.

Although the dividing wall between Jew and Gentile has been broken down, this does not mean that God has abandoned Israel. He cares for them as he does for all ethnic groups and promises they will be present in glory. Paul says he is proof God has not forgotten his people (Romans 11:1).

So the mission of the later harvest is to all nations. The message is the still, small voice of Christ speaking to the believer what he must in turn loudly proclaim to the world. And the method is to be Christ's representative, for whatever is done to the disciple is done to Jesus.

Timeline of the Three Harvests

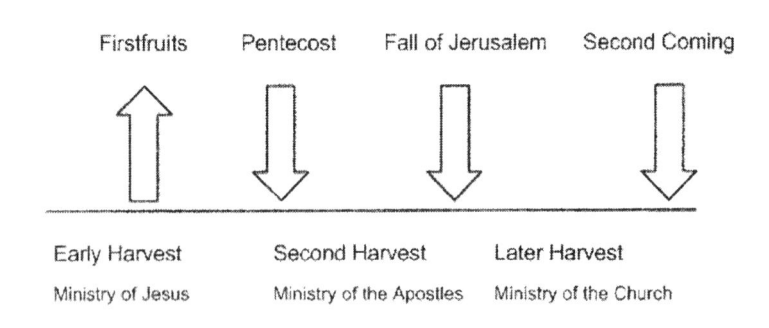

Firstfruits	Pentecost	Fall of Jerusalem	Second Coming
⬆	⬇	⬇	⬇

Early Harvest	Second Harvest	Later Harvest
Ministry of Jesus	Ministry of the Apostles	Ministry of the Church

The Feast of Firstfruits marked the beginning of harvesting for the year. But it was only after a sheaf of grain was waved before the Lord as an offering recognizing his gracious gift of the harvest that anyone could enjoy any of the crops. Likewise, even though the disciples and others believed on Jesus during his lifetime, no one was truly saved until Christ died on the cross. When he arose on the feast of

Firstfruits, he was that first sheaf offered up to God, opening up the enjoyment of eternal life to all who trust in him.

With the arrival of the Spirit on Pentecost we entered into the second harvest. This was a period of about 40 years of grace as God waited on Israel to acknowledge their Messiah. Jesus denounced the Jewish leaders and called out to the rebellious city of Jerusalem, pleading with them to respond to his loving call. But they refused.

> *You serpents, you brood of vipers, how are you to escape being sentenced to hell? Therefore I send you prophets and wise men and scribes, some of whom you will kill and crucify, and some you will flog in your synagogues and persecute from town to town, so that on you may come all the righteous blood shed on earth, from the blood of innocent Abel to the blood of Zechariah the son of Barachiah, whom you murdered between the sanctuary and the altar. Truly, I say to you, all these things will come upon this generation.*
>
> *O Jerusalem, Jerusalem, the city that kills the prophets and stones those who are sent to it! How often would I have gathered your children together as a hen gathers her brood under her wings, and you would not! See, your house is left to you desolate.*
>
> **Matthew 23:33-38**

Here we see the posture of the second harvest. It is an impassioned plea to the people of Israel to accept their Messiah. But during this time there was increasing hostility toward the followers of Jesus until God's judgment of destruction rained down on Jerusalem and the nation of Israel in 70 A.D.

Since that time we have been in the later harvest as salvation is trumpeted to all nations, spreading the gospel into all the world that men might be saved from every language, people, nation, tribe, and tongue.

As we expected, therefore, the first two harvests were fulfilled in the first century. We presently live in the time of the later harvest, which will not be complete until Christ returns to utterly defeat all opposition to his absolute reign.

Chapter 12: The Divine Plan

For the Lord GOD does nothing without revealing his secret to his servants the prophets.

Amos 3:7

In this passage, the prophet Amos gives a basic principle by which God operates. God is like the champion billiard player who can call his shots ahead of time and then make them happen exactly as he described it. He announces his intentions beforehand and then accomplishes them, displaying his absolute sovereignty over all history. And that is what he has done with the feasts of Israel. Centuries in advance, God established the feasts as a type of performance "pre-enacting" just how he would go about mending his broken world.

Jesus fulfilled the first four feasts of Israel in the first century.

- He died on the cross as the perfect **Passover** Lamb, freeing us from death and slavery to sin by his shed blood.

- He consecrated us to himself by making us his righteousness and by winning the war of heaven, fulfilling the **Feast of Unleavened Bread**.

- He rose again on the third day as the **Firstfruits** from the dead.

- And he poured out his Spirit at **Pentecost**, guaranteeing our salvation and empowering his church to extend his kingdom.

While Christ completely fulfilled what the first four feasts predicted in the first century, he has only partially fulfilled the prophecies of the remaining festivals. Each of the last three feasts is already and not yet. Some aspects have already been accomplished in Christ, while other aspects await fulfillment at the end of time.

- Christ has been crowned King and sat down on his throne in fulfillment of the **Feast of Trumpets**. But the trumpet warning calling all men to salvation that has been blaring from the first century will not stop until the second coming. So the Feast of Trumpets is only partially fulfilled.

- Through the cross Jesus entered the Most Holy Place with his own blood to make atonement for men, fulfilling what the first goat of the **Day of Atonement** predicted. Therefore, we have been rescued from the penalty of sin. But we are yet to be set free from the presence of sin. That aspect of Atonement awaits complete fulfillment on Judgment Day when the wicked who reject Christ's salvation are sent away forever just like the second goat on the Day of Atonement.

- Finally, we today enjoy the blessings of fellowship with God as his Holy Spirit has been sent into our hearts. Yet we still look forward to the day when our faith will be sight, when God has taken up residence with us on the new earth. We are already new creations in Christ, but we do not yet see the natural world restored as a new creation. This will all come to fruition when the **Feast of Tabernacles** is finally and completely fulfilled.

The feasts emphasize that our salvation is not just a ticket to heaven. The assurance of heaven after this life is only the beginning of our salvation. Every believer needs to see the scope of God's redemption laid out in the seven feasts.

When Christ, our perfect **Passover** Lamb, took our punishment upon himself, he made it possible for a holy Judge to declare us not guilty. This is justification. Since our sin is no longer counted against us, God can welcome us into his presence. We can go to heaven. But that is not all.

Justification leads to sanctification as we are not only acquitted of our crimes but are dressed in the righteousness of Christ. God the Judge looks on us not as criminals sprung from prison on a technicality, but as his own perfect, beloved Son. As believers justified before God we are formed into the body of Christ and are empowered to grow more and more into his likeness. As the **Feast of Unleavened Bread** featured the removal of leaven, Christ's sacrifice has removed the penalty of sin from us and has begun the process of removing the power of sin over us. Salvation is not just a destination in heaven, it is victory in this life over the sin that destroys us.

Then Jesus rose on the third day as the **Firstfruits** from the dead, assuring those who are justified by his death and sanctified to be his righteousness of also sharing in his resurrection. We, too, will be glorified as he is. Heaven will not be a disembodied, blissful existence floating around on a cloud, strumming a harp. We look forward to a resurrection body just like Christ's that will not be constrained by sin, pain, and mortal limitations. We will be freed to fully live according to God's original design.

If we stopped with the first three feasts we could conclude that salvation is all for our individual benefit. God saves me from sin to give me a home in heaven, empowers me to resist temptation like Christ, and promises to raise me up in a new and improved immortal body. The **Feast of Pentecost** clarifies that the blessings of justification, sanctification, and glorification are not the sum total of our salvation. God came to dwell within us to empower those he has saved to continue advancing his kingdom toward its goal. That kingdom began in Jerusalem as Jesus predicted and spread to Judea, Samaria, and the ends of the earth. Salvation is not just about me, it is about re-establishing God's kingdom on earth.

But the kingdom is not complete until every knee bows and every tongue confesses that Jesus is Lord (Philippians 2:10-11). As the **Feast of Trumpets** indicates, we are called to trumpet the message of the reigning King and his coming kingdom. We not only look forward to the kingdom, we also participate in bringing it into existence. We stand in this world as evidence of the pardon available to sinners, as examples of the fellowship God wishes to restore with those made in his image, and as emissaries sharing the good news of salvation.

The **Day of Atonement** illustrates the awesome privilege afforded those who trust in Jesus. By the offer of his blood, Christ has opened the way into the Most Holy Place, the very presence of God. The believer can confidently enter in, but not simply for his own benefit. The coming Judgment Day when all sin is put away forever is pictured by the banishment of the second goat. We enter the Lord's presence to pray for his coming kingdom and to receive instructions for its advancement. Salvation is so much more than a ticket to heaven, it is an invitation into the power center of the universe!

There is really a threefold fulfillment of the **Feast of Tabernacles**. First, the Word became flesh and tabernacled among us. God the Son put off his heavenly glory and walked this earth as a man. He demonstrated his desire for fellowship and then provided the means for people to enter that fellowship through his death on the cross. Next, because of Christ's sacrifice the Spirit was poured out, taking up residence in the hearts of believers. Far from being simply an invitation allowing us entrance into a good party in the afterlife, salvation means having a real connection with God here and now. Finally, the ultimate goal of redemption is when the dwelling of God is with men as the state of perfection that existed in the Garden of Eden is restored.

At the beginning of this book we noted that the feasts are the recipe God wrote down in advance and that he follows to save his creation. Thus, God's recipe for redeeming his fallen world is:

- Crucify one perfect **Passover** Lamb to save from sin.

- Sprinkle in 7 days of **Unleavened Bread** to form people into Christ's righteousness.

- Raise Jesus' body as the **Firstfruits** from the dead to defeat death.

- Pour out the Holy Spirit at **Pentecost** to empower God's people to live out Christ's righteousness.

- Spread this mixture out all over the world with **Trumpets**, announcing Christ's reign and inviting people into his kingdom. Bake for an unspecified time known only by the Father.

- Top off with the **Day of Atonement** to remove all infecting sin.

- Serve and enjoy in **Tabernacles** forever, in direct fellowship with the Lord of the universe.

God was very particular in how he commanded his people to observe his feasts because they are the recipe for redemption. The feasts explain our salvation and God's program for redeeming his rebellious creation. Pay attention to the feasts, they are the framework for the future.

Appendix: Tables of Sacrifices

Daily Sacrifice
Numbers 28:3-8

Requirement	Meaning
1 lamb burnt offering in morning 1 lamb burnt offering at twilight	Continual reminder of ongoing consecration of Israel stemming from Passover that established them as God's special people

Weekly (Sabbath) Sacrifice
Numbers 28:9-10

Requirement	Meaning
2 lambs burnt offering (in addition to daily offering)	Intensification of daily offering for the special day of the week

Monthly Sacrifice*
Numbers 28:11-15

Requirement	Meaning
2 bulls burnt offering	Consecration of Israel and priests
1 ram burnt offering	Christ our substitute
7 lambs burnt offering	Consecration of Gentile church
1 goat sin offering	Atonement through blood of Christ

*Also each of 7 days of Unleavened Bread (Numbers 28:19-24) and on Pentecost (Numbers 28:27-30)

Pentecost Sacrifice*
Leviticus 23:18-19

Requirement	Meaning
7 lambs burnt offering	Consecration of Gentile church
1 bull burnt offering	Ordination of priests (the church)
2 rams burnt offering	Ordination of priests (the church)
1 goat sin offering	Atonement through blood of Christ
2 lambs fellowship offering	Fellowship with God through indwelling Spirit

*Companion to 2 loaves and in addition to standard monthly offering

Sacrifice Unique to Fall Feasts*
Numbers 29:2-5, 8-11, 36-38

Requirement	Meaning
1 bull burnt offering	Consecration of Israel
1 ram burnt offering	Christ our substitute
7 lambs burnt offering	Consecration of Gentile church
1 goat sin offering	Atonement through blood of Christ

*Feast of Trumpets, Day of Atonement, Feast of Tabernacles

Made in the USA
Columbia, SC
21 September 2017